PRAISE FOR
THE COMPASS WITHIN

"Arguably life's most important concept brilliantly shared within an absolutely beautifully written story! This book—destined to be a classic—should not only be a treasured part of your personal and business library; it should be studied until its wisdom is part of your very being. Then buy a copy for everyone you love who you would like to see live a happier and more fulfilled life, and for every team member whose potential you'd like to help develop to its fullest."

—Bob Burg, bestselling coauthor of *The Go-Giver*

"Glazer has written a winner! *The Compass Within* is more than excellent storytelling—it's a timeless parable that illustrates the power of living and leading in alignment with your core values."

—Patrick Lencioni, *New York Times* bestselling author of *The Five Dysfunctions of a Team* and *The Advantage*

"Robert Glazer's *The Compass Within* beautifully guides readers to do the introspective work needed to truly live authentically and stay true to their values. His breakthrough book demonstrates conclusively that living in accordance with your core values aligns who we are with the decisions we make in our work, relationships, and communities."

—Bill George, Harvard Business School Executive Fellow, author of *True North*, and former Chair and CEO of Medtronic

"Glazer's engaging parable illustrates how defining and aligning with core values leads to better choices and a more fulfilling life. *The Compass Within* is a must-read for anyone looking to make the big decisions in life with confidence and clarity."

—Annie Duke, *New York Times* bestselling author of *Quit* and *Thinking in Bets*

"Robert Glazer's *The Compass Within* is a powerful exploration of aligning personal and professional life with core values, delivered through an engaging and relatable narrative. This book masterfully combines introspection and actionable guidance, much like Patrick Lencioni's *The Five Dysfunctions of a Team* or Simon Sinek's *Start With Why*. With its storytelling approach, it resonates deeply, offering readers a framework for uncovering their values and making choices that foster authentic fulfillment. Glazer's insight and empathy shine through, making this an essential read for anyone seeking clarity and alignment in a complex and distressing world."

—Jerry Colonna, author of *Reunion: Leadership and the Longing to Belong* and *Reboot: Leadership and the Art of Growing Up*

"In a world full of noise and uncertainty, *The Compass Within* is the ultimate guide to clarity and purpose. This life-changing book provides the tools to make decisions with confidence and live a life of meaning and impact."

—Jesse Cole, Founder and CEO of the Savannah Bananas and bestselling author of *Fans First* and *Find Your Yellow Tux*

"*The Compass Within* is a must-read for anyone seeking deeper self-awareness, fulfillment, and alignment at work and in life."

—Tasha Eurich, *New York Times* bestselling author of *Shatterproof*, *Insight*, and *Bankable Leadership*

"*The Compass Within* is a gripping parable that will challenge everything you thought you knew about success and fulfillment. A must-read."

—Harry Kraemer Jr., former CEO of Baxter International and Professor of Leadership at Northwestern's Kellogg School of Management

"A must-read journey into self-discovery and values-driven living; this book is a game-changer for everyone from the student to the CEO."

—Asheesh Advani, CEO of Junior Achievement and author of *Modern Achievement*

"If you have that nagging feeling that you have not yet fulfilled your potential, *The Compass Within* could be the book you've been looking for!"

—Brian Scudamore, Founder and CEO of 1–800-GOT-JUNK? and author of *WTF?! (Willing to Fail)*

"*The Compass Within* has the power to transform! Glazer delivers a narrative that is both relatable and powerful and provides a framework that will help you align your core values with their decisions. If you want to lead with authenticity and unlock potential in yourself and others, this book is your foundation."

—Liz Wiseman, bestselling author of *Multipliers* and *Impact Players* and CEO of the Wiseman Group

ALSO BY
ROBERT GLAZER

*Elevate: Push Beyond Your Limits and
Unlock Success in Yourself and Others*

*Elevate Your Team: Empower Your Team
to Reach Their Full Potential and Build
a Business That Builds Leaders*

*How to Thrive in the Virtual Workplace:
Simple and Effective Tips for Successful,
Productive, and Empowered Remote Work*

*Friday Forward: Inspiration & Motivation to
End Your Week Stronger Than It Started*

*Rethinking Two Weeks' Notice:
Changing the Way Employees Leave
Companies for the Better*

For more information, visit
www.robertglazer.com/book.

THE COMPASS WITHIN

**A LITTLE STORY ABOUT
THE VALUES THAT GUIDE US**

ROBERT GLAZER

Copyright © 2025 by Robert Glazer and Elevate Media Group, LLC.
Cover and internal design © 2025 by Sourcebooks
Cover design by Pete Garceau
Cover images © TA2YO4NORI/Getty Images
Internal design by Laura Boren
Internal images © appleuzr/Getty Images

Sourcebooks and the colophon are registered trademarks of Sourcebooks.

All rights reserved. No part of this book may be reproduced in any form or by any electronic or mechanical means including information storage and retrieval systems—except in the case of brief quotations embodied in critical articles or reviews—without permission in writing from its publisher, Sourcebooks.

No part of this book may be used or reproduced in any manner for the purpose of training artificial intelligence technologies or systems.

This publication is designed to provide accurate and authoritative information in regard to the subject matter covered. It is sold with the understanding that the publisher is not engaged in rendering legal, accounting, or other professional service. If legal advice or other expert assistance is required, the services of a competent professional person should be sought. —*From a Declaration of Principles Jointly Adopted by a Committee of the American Bar Association and a Committee of Publishers and Associations*

Published by Sourcebooks
1935 Brookdale RD, Naperville, IL 60563-2773
(630) 961-3900
sourcebooks.com

Cataloging-in-Publication Data is on file with the Library of Congress.

Printed and bound in Canada.
FR 10 9 8 7 6 5 4 3 2 1

For those courageous enough to make the sacrifices and tough decisions required to live a life in alignment with their values. And to Ollie, for giving our family a decade of unconditional love and snuggles.

CONTENTS

INTRODUCTION — XIII

1. **The Conversation** — **1**
2. **The Disconnects** — **37**
3. **The Questions** — **71**
4. **The Discovery** — **105**
5. **The Values** — **133**
6. **The Big Three** — **150**
7. **The Lesson** — **175**

CORE VALUES COURSE — 208

ACKNOWLEDGMENTS — 210

NOTES — 213

ABOUT THE AUTHOR — 214

INTRODUCTION

We all aspire to live as our most authentic selves in every space that we are in—in our relationships, our work, and our communities. But we often feel a disconnect or tension between who we are and the people around us.

Like most people, you've probably experienced times when you and your partner just weren't on the same page. These moments can feel jarring and unsettling. While you don't want to turn minor disagreements into major problems, you occasionally worry that the two of you have fundamentally different worldviews. The question is how to distinguish between a normal source of tension, which can be resolved through communication and compromise, and a deeper, potentially irresolvable conflict.

Similarly, you may find yourself adapting your personality or lifestyle to fit into your community in a way that feels inauthentic and draining. This can lead to engaging in activities, conversations, or debates that feel superficial or forced. For instance, you might often go out to bars, shop at expensive boutiques, or eat at the latest trendy places when you'd rather be hiking with friends, discussing books, cooking and entertaining at home, or spending time on creative projects. Or maybe it is the other way around. If the people in your social group show no interest in exploring new music and culinary sensations, you might find yourself stuck in a routine that drains your energy and stifles your enthusiasm. Consider whether the community where you live makes it easier to be yourself or if you are regularly pulled into activities and opinions that don't feel authentic to the person you are.

This dissonance isn't limited to our personal lives.

INTRODUCTION

Have you ever received a request from a superior that makes you wince, and you perform the task requested of you only reluctantly? Perhaps you have been part of a corporate initiative filled with jargon or a coldly executed layoff in which you participated only with a heavy heart. You may not be able to articulate *why* you felt so uncomfortable; you just know that something didn't sit right. Maybe you went along to avoid conflict but still found yourself dwelling on it later, trying to make sense of your discomfort. This is natural. Today, the expectation that we will simply toe the company line is dated. Security and salary are no longer the only defining factors of a good job; we crave roles that feel meaningful.

All these examples point to a larger issue: a misalignment between the roles expected of us and our core values. Most of us are fortunate to live in a world where we are free to express our deepest values. When we succeed in aligning our lives with those values, we feel a sense of peace and enthusiasm, as if we were truly living our ideal lives. In contrast, the discomfort caused by a misalignment of values is deep and painful and rarely fades with time; and if it does fade, it's usually due to self-abandonment, giving up on the belief that we will ever be able to forge a life in accordance with those values.

Defining these elusive core values is challenging for both people and organizations. Many corporations proudly display company values that look good on the wall but may be hard to reconcile with the behavior of employees. Or they may espouse values that are so vague that they apply universally without defining any specific behaviors. Who doesn't want to "strive for excellence" or "be a great team member"?

With more mobility and choice than ever, we want to walk into work feeling that the job we do and the people we work with are aligned with our values on a fundamental level. The same is true of the communities we choose to live in and the people we select as partners. Aligning our lives with our values is the key to any healthy long-lasting relationship, at work, in a romantic context, or in our social lives.

INTRODUCTION

To live by our core values, we need to understand them. The question is how can we do this? How can we be sure exactly what we value and then articulate those values clearly enough to guide both the important decisions in our lives and our day-to-day choices?

For many, the search ends at these questions because they simply don't know how to find these answers. This book offers the guide you need to get clarity on your core values and start aligning your life with them.

The journey of uncovering and living core values is exceptionally worthwhile, though often filled with complication and uncertainty. After years of trial and error, I believe that I have established a system to help people do this definitively, zeroing in on the previously hidden drives and motivations that form the foundation of our deepest fulfillment or that cause us the greatest pain.

We all have an internal compass that guides our behavior and shapes the decisions we make: where we choose to make our home, how we construct our careers, and with whom we share our lives. Clarifying the messages of this inner compass is one of the most powerful methods I know for determining the answers to the biggest questions we face in life.

I speak from experience here. In my own life, figuring out what matters most to me and shaping those insights into defined values that I can consistently reference have been the very foundation of my personal and professional development. I even divide my life into "before" and "after" my core-values discovery. I went from attaining a modest degree of success in my early career to discovering a leadership style that felt authentic and uniquely mine, and from where I was able to communicate exactly what mattered most to me and why. This not only enabled me to make better decisions for myself, my family, and my career; it allowed me to reach my innate personal and professional potential for the first time. I embarked on this journey largely on my own initiative, which made the process longer and more difficult than I hope it will be for you.

Determining our core values is not an exercise in

deciding what we aspire to achieve. It's a matter of uncovering patterns that have existed for years, even if we haven't been able to see them clearly or connect the dots. In many cases, closely held values are forged through formative life experiences, often in childhood or adolescence. We naturally gravitate toward emulating the values we resonated with when we were young while striving at all costs to avoid and counteract those past experiences that created pain or went against our sense of self.

In the coming pages, I will share the process for living in alignment with your core values. You'll follow the story of a fictional manager, Jamie Hynes, as he goes through his own journey of core-values discovery and compare his experiences with your own. As he navigates big choices about his career, his partner, and where to make his home, you may recognize some of your own values in him or be prompted to a similar revelation about what matters most to you.

I chose to offer a framework for your own personal inquiry in the form of a parable because it's more effective and memorable to show this process than to tell it. The purpose of Jamie's story is not to endorse particular values, but to illuminate the process of discovery. The pages ahead will not make any judgment about what your values should be nor promote specific right or wrong answers to the questions posed in this book. You may disagree with some of Jamie's conclusions and decisions, and that disagreement may very well reveal something about your own values. In the conclusion to this book, I will recap Jamie's journey and explicitly share the process and the tools he follows in the story, which you can use to recreate his experience for yourself.

As you read along, I hope you'll find yourself empathizing with Jamie's journey and reflecting on what you would do in his situation. While I hope you will enjoy the story on its own merits, my greater ambition is that by the time you finish it, you'll gain a new perspective on what brings you enjoyment and fulfillment, igniting a curiosity to discover and live by your own core values and be guided by the compass within.

1

THE CONVERSATION

The time was just after 4:00 p.m. on a typically dark, dreary January day in Boston as Jamie Hynes exited the corner conference room at Jones Communications. His six-month performance review had turned into another in a long line of frustrating conversations with his boss, Matt Embers. With his head hanging, Jamie trudged back to his desk, neglecting to smile or say hello to anyone along the way.

Jamie wore his emotions on his sleeve, and his agitated state was obvious to anyone paying attention. Deep in his own thoughts, a gnawing pit in his stomach, he stared out the window beside his desk, eyeing the last glimmer of daylight on the horizon, half-obscured by a flurry of snowflakes.

Jamie flipped open his laptop and started typing absent-mindedly but quickly realized he was too exasperated to be truly productive. Sitting in his cubicle, he replayed in his mind the conversation he'd just had with Matt, a managing partner at Jones. Revisiting it only darkened his mood further until he felt as gloomy as the Boston skyline. As he pondered his next move, a light bulb went on in his mind. He suddenly realized that there was one person he very much did want to talk to about his predicament: Chloe Hitchcock.

Jamie had first met Chloe the previous year when they found themselves in the same breakout group at a meeting of the Emerging Sales and Marketing Leaders (ESML) forum, an invite-only mastermind group for up-and-coming sales and marketing professionals in the Greater Boston area. At twenty-eight, Jamie was hitting his stride in his career, and he and Chloe quickly became fast friends and confidants.

He needed a gut check on what had just happened, so he texted her right away. Hey Chloe, can you chat? Did not go well today.

His phone buzzed almost immediately: I've got a pitch. Can I call you tonight?

Sure, he replied. Just ping me when you can. Would love to get your take on something, thanks!

For a few moments, Jamie stared vacantly at the screen of his phone, uncertain what to do next. Then, coming back to reality, he realized it had already been a long day and he was more than ready to go home. He packed up his laptop, bundled himself up against the bitter weather, and plodded downstairs toward the exit.

As Jamie passed through the Jones Communications lobby, he happened to glance up at the Jones Core Values, painted in large, ornate red letters on the blue wall, representing the company colors. The words were displayed prominently above the main entrance to the firm's headquarters. He had walked by them countless times without really registering their meaning.

OUR CORE VALUES:

- Respect
- Integrity
- Win as a Team
- Clients First
- Excellence Always

As he gazed at the words, it occurred to Jamie for the first time that he hadn't heard the core values spoken aloud since his orientation at the company nearly three years earlier. For all their prominence in the lobby, the values felt particularly hollow after Jamie's conversation with Matt Embers. He scoffed—quietly, even though he was alone—at the difference between the words on the wall and the company he had come to know.

A cold burst of air chilled Jamie as he stepped outside. With his head bowed to shield his face from the worst of the wind, he headed to the nearby parking garage. Following a frigid ten-minute walk, he unlocked his ten-year-old Honda CRV and began to warm up in the front seat. It didn't take long for him to start ruminating once again on his meeting with Matt and from there to reflect on his time at Jones preceding that fateful conversation. As he pulled out of the garage and set off on the fifty-minute drive to his home in Westville, Jamie was deep in thought.

Running over the sequence of events in his mind, Jamie found himself recalling his first few days at Jones after he started as a fresh-faced senior associate three years earlier. Jamie had always wanted to work in PR, and he was highly excited to land a job at Jones, which commanded a sterling reputation within the industry. After meeting the company's namesake founder, Mark Jones, and learning about the firm's values and history, Jamie quickly realized how lucky he was to be placed on Stacey Smith's team.

When Jamie met her, Stacey was a director at Jones, universally acknowledged as a rising star and well respected throughout the company. Jamie collaborated with Stacey on the surging channels of social media and influencer marketing—relatively new practices within the company's larger scope—working closely with some of the firm's biggest clients.

Jamie vividly remembered one of his first meetings with Stacey. They were preparing for a pitch to Rocket Biosciences, one of the firm's largest, fastest-growing clients. Even at that early stage in their relationship, he had noticed that she was always prepared and insightful, with a knack for asking the right questions and drawing out innovative ideas.

"I've read your analysis on the current trends in social media," she told him, her eyes focused and attentive. "Your approach is fresh, and I think it's exactly what we need. Let's build on it for the pitch."

This encouragement boosted Jamie's confidence, and they spent hours refining their strategy. As they collaborated more, Jamie realized this type of mentorship was not a one-off; it was an integral part of Stacey's leadership style. Her dedication to excellence and genuine interest in his development were evident in every interaction.

Under Stacey's guidance, Jamie earned two promotions in his very first year at Jones. During his second year with the company, he was promoted a third time, to the role of associate director, which offered a salary in excess of $100,000. This was particularly fulfilling, as hitting that six-figure threshold was a goal he had set for himself years earlier and achieved ahead of schedule.

While he undoubtedly benefited from Stacey's support, Jamie's talent for marketing was apparent from the start. After one of Jamie's first client meetings, Stacey praised how he listened intently as the client described their challenges, his eyes never leaving theirs. He nodded thoughtfully, summarized what he'd heard, then began to outline a strategy that seamlessly blended an original perspective with a strategic approach, making the client feel understood and valued.

His ability to connect with people was evident in the way he could turn even the most casual conversation into a productive dialogue. One afternoon, while walking ahead to lunch with a potential client before Stacey arrived to join the meeting, Jamie effortlessly steered the discussion toward the client's goals, subtly weaving in his own insights and ideas. By the time they reached the restaurant, the client was so impressed they were ready to sign a contract.

On top of these qualities, Jamie exhibited a dedication to his work. He often stayed late, poring over case studies and marketing trends, and scheduled regular one-on-one sessions with Stacey to pick her brain and build his capacity. His people skills and dedication to continuous learning made Jamie a rare double threat: an employee who could both deliver exceptional results and build strong, lasting relationships with clients.

He was told his future at the company was bright, and Stacey consistently rated him a top performer. With this encouragement, Jamie had hoped he might have the opportunity to become a partner at Jones one day.

But then, just over two years into Jamie's tenure with Jones, things took an abrupt turn.

THE CONVERSATION

One Monday afternoon, Stacey asked Jamie if he was free to chat for a few minutes, just as Jamie was finishing his day. When he nodded in agreement, she led him into the company's corner conference room. This in itself was hardly unusual; they used the conference room regularly to escape the open bullpen of desks, utilizing the quieter atmosphere and the one-on-one time to solve a client issue or brainstorm new campaigns on the whiteboard.

On this occasion, however, he immediately felt a sense of unease. Something about the expression on Stacey's face as she requested his time unnerved him, and as she walked in front of him toward the conference room, he thought her shoulders looked unusually tight. Involuntarily, the hair stood up on the back of his neck, and he instinctively wondered whether he was about to receive some bad news.

After they entered the room, Stacey closed the door behind them, something she rarely did. Then she invited Jamie to sit down and pulled up a chair opposite him.

"Are you firing me?" he joked, masking his anxiety with a playful smile.

Stacey shook her head no and laughed, but he sensed a strained undertone in her voice.

"What's going on, Stacey?" Jamie asked. "You look like you've just seen a ghost. You're making me nervous."

"Well, I have some good news and some bad news," Stacey replied. "Which do you want first?"

"You know our rule with clients," Jamie reminded her. "Always the bad news first."

"I'm leaving Jones," she said quietly. "Today is my last day."

Even though he was sitting, Jamie felt like someone had simultaneously swept his legs out from under him and punched him in the stomach.

"What? Why?" Jamie could barely muster an audible reply as he struggled to process this unexpected news.

Stacey took a deep breath before she spoke, and Jamie noticed a conflicted look on her face, as though she were battling competing internal impulses. He sensed relief but also something else—a look of wistfulness that reminded him of his mom's face when he was a teenager boarding the bus to overnight camp and she was a proud yet concerned parent, waving him farewell.

"I just felt that it was time for me to try something different," she said. "I love the work I do, and I love my team. But I'm not sure Jones is the best place for me long-term. I'm going to a company where I'll be a little more…" Stacey hesitated for a few seconds, clearly choosing her final word carefully. "Aligned," she finished.

Jamie had never heard Stacey gossip or speak poorly of her colleagues at Jones, including her boss, Matt Embers. Quite the opposite, in fact; she went out of her way to support him. Jamie recalled a specific incident six months after he joined the team, when Matt's team had mistakenly sent an incorrect bill to a new client, which drew an incredulous reply from the client and started the relationship on a bad note. In a conversation with Jamie, Stacey addressed the issue directly but refused to cast blame. "These things happen," she said calmly. "We're a team, and we just need to earn their trust back with our great work." Stacey's refusal to speak poorly of others was a quality Jamie admired greatly.

Jamie had witnessed Stacey extend the same courtesy to her clients, who were often very demanding. He recalled a particular meeting where a client, clearly frustrated, spoke rudely and pushed boundaries with their requests. Jamie could see the tension in Stacey's eyes, yet she maintained her composure.

"Thank you for your feedback," Stacey had said in a steady voice. "Let's work together to find a solution that meets your needs." After the meeting, Jamie asked her if she was bothered by the client's behavior. Stacey simply smiled. "It's part of the job. Our focus should always be on delivering our best, regardless of the circumstances." Her ability to conduct herself with dignity, even in challenging situations, was a testament to her professionalism and integrity.

Given these circumstances, Stacey's unusual admission about alignment alarmed Jamie. He knew he wasn't getting the full story and suspected Stacey didn't want to taint his perspective on Jones.

Jamie was aware of the extensive politics at Jones, but Stacey had purposefully shielded him from most of them, keeping him focused on his clients and career. On one of their projects, Matt and the sales team had gotten into a heated argument over who should get credit for a major client expansion. When Jamie asked Stacey about it, she brushed it off, saying, "It's not a big deal. They'll figure it out." It was only when Jamie mentioned the situation to a fellow associate that he got a fuller picture.

"You're lucky, Jamie," the associate had said. "Stacey's shielding you from a lot. This goes on all the time with our team." This revelation made Jamie appreciate Stacey even more, recognizing her efforts to protect him from distractions and guide his career growth.

As he thought back to that moment, Jamie wondered what else was going on beneath the surface of Stacey's outward calm. He tried to interpret her remark about alignment and compare it to the expression on her face. "Where are you going?"

"I'm going in-house to lead marketing at Sugar Hill Diagnostics," she replied.

Sugar Hill was a former Jones client and a coveted unicorn, a nickname given to start-ups accruing more than $1 billion in value. The leadership at Sugar Hill had loved Stacey but terminated the relationship with Jones the previous year following a falling-out between their VP of marketing and Matt Embers. Jamie didn't know exactly how things had played out and was suddenly intensely curious to know the details of what had transpired. He knew Stacey wouldn't share them, but he surmised that if she was making the leap from Jones to Sugar Hill, there must be a good reason.

"Can you take me with you?" he asked, realizing as he said it that he was only half-joking.

"You know I would in a second, Jamie," Stacey assured him. "But I signed a nonsolicitation agreement when I joined, so I can't hire you as an employee for at least a year.

However, that also leads me on to the good news," she added, smiling broadly and looking fully like her usual self for the first time since she had approached him for a conversation. "I recommended to Matt that you be promoted to director as my replacement. You know the clients and have their trust. Matt agreed wholeheartedly, and the job is yours."

A huge smile lit up Jamie's face, washing away the concern he had felt moments earlier.

"Holy shit," he exclaimed, unsure whether he'd said it in his head or out loud.

Since he had first joined Jones, Jamie had badly wanted to be a director. He had discussed the prospect extensively with his forum at ESML and made a list of all the steps he would need to take to get there. In his mind, the opportunity was at least two to three years away, but suddenly, without warning, it had arrived. At twenty-nine, he would be the youngest director at the firm, a position in which he could earn more than $200,000 a year in total compensation, with sales bonuses, 401(k) matching, and profit sharing. As he digested the news, Jamie felt slightly dazed; it seemed as though Stacey were simultaneously abandoning him and hitting the fast-forward button on his career.

In addition to the professional advancement, the role would mean a lot to Jamie's personal life. He and his fiancée, Beth, were getting married next fall and hoping to start a family not too long after, which meant deciding on where they wanted to settle down and buy a home. Jamie being a director would be a game changer for them, broadening their options considerably.

"Really?" he said once his thoughts stopped racing.

"Really," Stacey replied.

"Wow, Stacey, I don't know what to say."

"You'd better say yes, or Matt will kill me," Stacey joked. "I went out on a limb for you."

Having fully absorbed the news of Stacey's departure and his unanticipated promotion, it dawned on Jamie that she had mentioned she was leaving immediately, meaning these were her final few hours at Jones.

"Stacey," he asked, "why are you leaving today? Shouldn't you give some kind of notice?" he asked.

"I actually did," she replied. "I offered to stay on for four weeks and help wind up all my accounts and get them properly transitioned. However, when I told Matt the news this morning, he said he would get back to me after lunch. When we spoke again in the afternoon, he mentioned that the partners were very surprised by my decision and…" She paused, hesitating for a moment as if she were about to say more. Then, in a composed tone, she continued, "They asked if I could wrap up my work today, and Matt requested that I get my things together and turn in my laptop by 5:00 p.m."

"They're walking you out the door like a traitor? I don't get it!" Despite his outburst, Jamie did get it. He had seen this scenario play out many times before at Jones; he had just never imagined it would happen to Stacey. "How will your clients react?"

"Not well, I would guess," Stacey said with a playful smirk. "Especially when I'm not the one who is going to tell them. That'll be the first problem you'll have to solve as a director."

Despite his slight misgivings about the situation as a whole, Jamie couldn't help but grin at the mention of his new title.

Soon after, Jamie helped Stacey pack up a few boxes and walked with her out of the Jones lobby—she for the last time in her career and he for the last time as an associate director. Jamie couldn't help but notice some of their colleagues directing subtle looks of disapproval at her as they strode out of the office, as though she bore a scarlet letter. Clearly, the news had traveled fast.

Jamie was struck by a sense of irony. He knew from experience that the leadership at Jones didn't think twice about firing someone on the spot without any notice or warning. He recalled an incident a year earlier when a colleague who had worked tirelessly on a major campaign was let go abruptly with no explanation. The news had spread through the office like wildfire, leaving everyone on edge.

On more than one occasion, Jamie had seen the leadership react bitterly when anyone tried to depart Jones on their own terms. It saddened him to see that despite being one of the firm's top performers for years, Stacey was not spared this ignominy. She had always given the firm and her colleagues the utmost respect, yet when it came time for her to leave, that respect was clearly not reciprocated.

It made Jamie realize that there was no good way to leave Jones. The firm's leadership demanded loyalty and hard work but didn't return the same consideration when someone decided to move on, no matter how much respect they showed their team or the firm in the manner of their departure. Seeing Stacey, who had shielded him from so much office politics, face the same demeaning treatment deepened his appreciation for her integrity and dedication.

He walked with Stacey to her car. She unlocked the driver's door and placed the box of belongings that was all that remained of her time with Jones on the front passenger seat, then stood up to face him on the other side of the opened door. For a moment, he thought he detected an impulse to share something—advice? a warning?—with him. Then discretion won out, and she simply smiled and waved her good-bye.

"Don't be a stranger," Stacey said.

"I won't," Jamie replied. "Thank you for everything, Stacey."

With that, Stacey left, and Jamie officially began his new role as a director at Jones. He couldn't wait to tell Beth the news.

When Jamie got home that night, he could hardly contain his excitement.

"You won't believe what happened today!" he exclaimed to Beth before relaying the series of events that had led to his promotion and Stacey's departure.

"That's amazing, Jamie!" she exclaimed as she ran to give him a hug, "You so deserve this."

Jamie told her about his raise and how it would allow them to now start looking seriously for a house, as their apartment was starting to feel small with Beth working from home more often.

After their initial moment of celebration, Beth expressed some concern with the abruptness of Stacey's departure, knowing how well she was respected by everyone who worked with her. She also encouraged Jamie to exercise a little caution when it came to spending his new raise before it even hit his bank account. While he knew she was right on both accounts, he couldn't help but feel like she was raining on his parade just as the confetti started to fall.

Jamie first met Beth McCormick when mutual friends set them up on a blind date, and they immediately hit it off. Before long, they became a couple, and on their three-year anniversary, Jamie proposed to Beth in front of the restaurant in Boston's North End neighborhood where they'd had their first date. He had never been happier in his life.

Born and raised in Nashville, Beth came from a large traditional southern Catholic family, where she was the third of five siblings. She moved to Boston to attend Boston College, fell in love with the city, and pursued a job there after college. She'd worked at the same company since graduation: Beacon Hill Builds, a well-respected residential architecture firm, where she had recently been promoted to senior project manager.

Coming from a large family where she was the middle child, Beth was a natural peacemaker deft at navigating strong personalities. Her laid-back, flexible style perfectly complemented Jamie's intense drive and ambition. Beth preferred to follow others' leads—including Jamie's—rather than asserting her own opinion. Jamie liked to joke that with his type-A tendencies and her type-B approach to life, they often balanced each other out.

Friends had commented to Beth that she and Jamie were a surprising match, given their different personalities and even more disparate passions and interests. While Jamie loved to hike in the summers and ski in the winters, Beth, coming from the south, had never skied before she met Jamie and found it intimidating, although she was an avid runner and loved to sail.

They attempted to split the difference, finding new activities they could learn to love together—including biking and taking tennis lessons. Biking had stuck—when the weather was nice enough, they went on a regular ride each weekend. They also enjoyed cooking together, with Jamie in charge of picking new recipes to try.

Jamie and Beth's differences extended to intellectual interests. While both were voracious readers, they were drawn to very different genres. Beth loved fantasy, poetry, and novels, while Jamie hadn't read a fiction book since college and preferred historical biographies, business books, and self-improvement. Neither ever showed much interest in what the other was reading, so they rarely discussed their respective insights. At one point, Jamie tried to spearhead a couples book club with some of their friends, but he and Beth couldn't agree on a book to read, and the idea soon fizzled.

Jamie and Beth also had occasional disconnects on

the role Beth's family played in their lives. Beth's parents were often vocal about their opinions on Jamie and Beth's life choices, including several passive-aggressive comments about their decision to settle in the Boston area rather than move to Nashville, where Beth's parents and several of her siblings still lived. Jamie was particularly irritated when Beth's mother remarked, "Well, you'll certainly wish you lived closer to us when you start a family," and was disappointed that Beth brushed off the comment rather than expressing her love of the Boston area and the life they had built together there.

Tensions with Beth and her family had become more noticeable as Jamie and Beth began planning their wedding, which they'd been doing for about a year by the time Jamie became a director. One of the sticking points was the service. Beth's parents wanted them to be married at their local church in Nashville by the family's longtime priest, who officiated the weddings of Beth's older brother and sister. Both Jamie and Beth, on the other hand, had their hearts set on an outdoor wedding during the New

England summer. Jamie wanted his uncle, a justice of the peace, to officiate. Since his uncle knew Jamie and Beth well, Jamie felt it would make the ceremony more intimate.

Jamie felt that Beth tended to defer too much to her parents, who were generously footing the majority of the bill for the wedding and had made many of their preferences known. Sometimes, he grew frustrated with her peacemaking tendencies, feeling that she avoided advocating for herself—or for Jamie—with her family.

Despite these differences, Beth brought out the best in him. Her warmth and kindness provided an important sense of balance and perspective in his hard-charging life. But Jamie sometimes found himself wondering how these many differences might strain their relationship, especially once they were married and raising kids together.

The morning after Stacey's departure, Jamie had his first one-on-one meeting with Matt Embers. Matt was one of the company's four managing partners and the brother-in-law of Mark Jones, the firm's founder and managing director. His group oversaw several of the firm's largest clients, including the growing social media and influencer practice that Jamie would soon lead.

When Jamie had first met Matt shortly after he started at Jones, Matt seemed like an executive straight out of central casting: smooth-talking, in command, and quick on his feet. As he had become familiar with Matt's leadership style, however, Jamie had noticed a few chinks in the armor. Often, Matt lacked context about the actual work the team was doing; Jamie had sat through several meetings in which Matt eagerly threw around ideas that did not seem to fit with the client's goals or the team's agreed-upon strategy.

During a crucial pitch meeting with Rocket Biosciences, for example, Matt went off script and suggested a flashy social media campaign based on mass market influencer partnerships—despite knowing that Rocket preferred to focus on the efficacy of its clinical trials and the robust data supporting its results. Prior to the meeting, the team had agreed on a more data-driven approach, highlighting detailed case studies and patient testimonials, which Jamie knew would resonate better with the client. When Matt insisted on his idea, seemingly more concerned with showcasing his authority than winning over the client, it almost derailed the client relationship at an early stage.

On a different occasion, during an internal meeting in which Matt presented more misaligned ideas for a new business pitch, Jamie noticed the team nodding along in agreement—not because they concurred, but seemingly to placate him.

Later, Jamie asked a colleague why no one had voiced their concerns. The colleague sighed, "Matt's got his strengths, but he can be argumentative when challenged directly, so we pick our battles. When the stakes are lower, it's easier to just go along with him. This was just a brainstorming session: he won't even remember his idea tomorrow, and we are not going to use it anyway."

Clearly, the team's strategy of selective acquiescence was a way to manage Matt's more difficult traits while leveraging his strengths.

In fairness, Jamie had noticed that while Matt often missed the mark with creative ideas, he was in his element when focused on the "business of the business." He was a wizard with budgeting, billing, account margins, and staffing. He also knew how to hold firm with clients around contract renewals and how to push for price increases at the right time in the client life cycle.

Because of this, it wasn't a surprise that Matt's team was by far the most profitable at Jones. Matt was openly proud of that fact, and his fixation on the bottom line was appreciated by many, especially those on his team who benefited from a strong bonus pool and sales commissions.

Although he often disagreed with Matt, Jamie considered him to be a generally decent guy. Matt was married to his high school sweetheart and had two young children, and Jamie remembered thinking Matt had been very sweet with his kids after seeing them together at the Jones company picnic the previous summer.

Like many male executives of his generation, though, Matt occasionally seemed slow to catch on to advancing norms in the workplace. Occasionally, he made comments that, while they wouldn't have provoked a second glance in the 1990s, landed badly today.

Jamie had a vivid memory of their last off-site, at a hotel that was a converted firehouse. After a few drinks, Matt had jokingly asked who wanted to "show their skills on the fire pole," which prompted several seconds of uncomfortable silence. But because of Matt's position at the company—and his status as the founder's brother-in-law—no one actively pushed back. Jamie had never heard anything further about the comment and concluded that Matt likely wasn't given the feedback it warranted.

Matt was also a product of the larger culture at Jones, which hadn't adapted much to changing times. Most recently, the company's stance on working from home after COVID-19, which had dramatically increased the prevalence of remote work across the industry, struck Jamie as unnecessarily rigid. Even as remote work became more common than ever, management at Jones insisted that employees come into the office full-time, regardless of whether there was a clear work justification.

It was with these conflicting impressions jostling for space in his head that Jamie walked into Matt's office for his first one-on-one the day after Stacey left the company. As he shut the door behind him, he felt a blend of excitement and apprehension, but the worry quickly subsided as Matt greeted Jamie with a big smile and a congratulatory handshake.

"Congrats, Jamie! This is a big step for you, bud," he remarked. "I am really excited to see what you can do in your new role."

"Thank you," Jamie responded, feeling a twinge of guilt as he reflected on the series of events that had led to his promotion. "You can trust me to give you and Jones my best."

Matt jumped straight into business: "I contacted

Zach King at Rocket this morning and told him about Stacey's abrupt departure. He was a bit concerned with the big product launch coming up and your team's crucial role in that campaign. But he was very happy to hear that you would be taking the wheel. You'll need to hit the ground running, so you'll want to get a new account manager in place to take over from you ASAP so you can fully step into Stacey's role. Let's talk about who makes the most sense."

Jamie considered this combination of affability and practical support a good start, and he and Matt quickly jumped into brainstorming ideas for the new team as well as putting together plans for each of Stacey's accounts. They discussed the timing of Rocket's upcoming product launch—a breakthrough new allergy drug—and how to best ensure a smooth transition.

Matt also shared more context about the expense budget, monthly retainer, and profitability and growth of the accounts Jamie was taking over, all things he would be responsible for in his new role. He walked through the financials of each of the accounts in painstaking detail, which Jamie appreciated.

Jamie left the meeting feeling energized, with a new appreciation for Matt's financial wizardry. He was excited to learn from Matt and to study how he expertly pitched clients on new projects and expansions. As a director, Jamie knew he could benefit from working more closely with some of Jones's top leaders. Additionally, as he grew the sizes of his accounts, he was poised to reap financial rewards through the sales bonus that was now part of his compensation.

And indeed, Jamie's first several weeks working closely with Matt were promising. While Matt's management style was much more hands-off than Stacey's, Jamie's accounts were performing well, especially Rocket. They met weekly, and Matt was enthusiastic about Jamie's progress, especially his team's efficiency and consistently high billing rates. They even went out for the occasional lunch or happy hour together. Jamie was a bit surprised to discover that not only was he learning a ton from Matt about finance and operations, but he also genuinely enjoyed his company.

But not every aspect of the director role was positive. About a month into Jamie's time in the role, in one of their weekly meetings, he and Matt had their first dustup. Matt had found a discrepancy between the time sheet of one of Jamie's account managers and the amount billed to the client, which he brought to Jamie's attention.

Jamie had brought in a new employee, David Hardy, to take his place as a manager on the Rocket account as he elevated into Stacey's role. While the budget for David's account management role was ten hours a week, he was brand new to Rocket's account and also fairly new to Jones, meaning he had a lot to learn to get up to speed. Despite his best efforts, in his first month on the job, David spent about twenty hours a week on Rocket, double the allocated ten hours and, just as importantly, twice what an experienced manager, rather than a newcomer adapting to an abrupt transition, would have needed.

Because the extra time was a result of Jones's staffing

changes rather than an increase in Rocket's scope of work, Jamie told David not to bill Rocket beyond the contracted amount. Instead, the extra ten hours per week were billed to an internal account for client development. As a result of Jamie's decision, an unexpected operating expense of $10,000 for the unbillable time hit Matt's monthly profit-and-loss statement, and he wanted to know why.

Jamie explained his thought process: he believed the extra hours were due to internal staffing issues created by Stacey's departure, and it seemed wrong to charge Rocket for Jones's problem. Plus, he noted to Matt, the Rocket relationship was so important that it seemed counterproductive to potentially upset the client over $10,000.

Of course, Jamie also felt that Jones's leadership had exacerbated the staffing problems by forcing Stacey to leave immediately, creating a rushed transition. However, he kept that last observation to himself.

Matt was unconvinced by Jamie's reasoning.

"I hear you, Jamie. But the simple truth of this business is account teams change all the time, and staffing hours change along with them," Matt reasoned. "David did twenty hours of work a week, and anything that doesn't get billed to the account comes out of our pocket, which affects both of our bonuses. In my experience, big clients are used to these occasional overages. Rocket pays us over ninety thousand dollars a month company wide and just announced a one-hundred-million-dollar fundraising round. They aren't going to bat an eye about an extra ten thousand dollars, trust me. I know you mean well, but in cases like this that could impact our bottom line, you should come to me before making a decision, Jamie."

Ultimately, Jamie agreed to bill the extra hours to Rocket to appease his new boss, but the decision didn't sit well with him. A month later, when Zach King, Jamie's contact at Rocket, asked about the additional charges, Jamie didn't feel confident in his response. Still, Zach accepted the extra hours without putting up a fight, just as Matt predicted.

While Jamie understood Matt's point of view and

rationalized the decision in his head, deep down, he felt it was the wrong choice, even after Zach accepted the overage. The decision made him physically uncomfortable, and knowing that Matt didn't trust his judgment compounded the discomfort.

It would not be the last frustrating thing Jamie would be asked to do.

2

THE DISCONNECTS

As he drove home, Jamie reflected on the many conversations and events leading up to the day's performance review. As he did so, they took on a different complexion—not isolated disagreements, but a pattern of behavior. He was only pulled back to reality by the sight of a familiar sign: "You Are Now Entering Westville." Blinking, he realized he had driven most of the way home deep in thought when he probably should have been paying more attention to the road.

Westville is about thirty miles west of Boston. For much of its history, it had been a small, sleepy suburban town known for its charming town center, access to hiking trails, and large parcels of land. Over the previous decade, however, the town had changed rapidly, especially following the addition of a commuter rail stop in town, which made the commute to Boston possible in less than twenty-five minutes, about half the time it took to make the journey by car on Boston's clogged commuter routes. When he didn't have client meetings off-site, like he did that day, Jamie enjoyed making use of this fast, efficient mode of transportation. Westville—seemingly overnight—had become a hub for young professionals priced out of more expensive, better-known Boston-adjacent suburbs, such as Brookline, Cambridge, and Newton.

Westville's town center now featured popular restaurants and a growing arts-and-entertainment sector. A few major developers had paid attention to the trend and launched new communities in the town, including brand-new town houses and sprawling McMansions, the latter of which drew particular ire from longtime Westville residents.

Jamie and Beth had lived in Westville for the last year, having moved there from Cambridge when they got engaged to get to know the area before buying a house and settling down to have kids. They loved their town house and enjoyed the urban feel of the nearby town center. Charlie's, a corner bar, had become their standing Friday night dinner spot; and their dog, Fenway, loved his Sunday walks on the town's old railway trail. Westville seemed to have everything Jamie and Beth wanted—space, charm, and accessibility. But as they approached the end of their lease, Jamie began to nurse a few reservations.

First, there was a clear division between the town's longtime residents, who'd lived in the area for generations, and young professionals like Jamie and Beth who were moving in and slowly taking over. This schism manifested itself in many ways, including a very active political climate. At times, it seemed as though everyone felt a strong need to make their views clear to the whole community.

Jamie wasn't involved with either political party

and didn't align with the extremes. In the lead-up to the Massachusetts gubernatorial election the previous November, though, he had noticed that nearly every yard in Westville displayed a sign proclaiming support for one candidate or the other.

While the political fever in Westville seemed to break once the election was over, there were several other facets of local life that began to concern Jamie.

Neither Jamie nor Beth grew up poor by any definition of the word; both came from middle-class families with two working parents who espoused the value of saving and a strong work ethic. They had each worked throughout high school and college and, even then, had taken out student loans to make ends meet. Since college, they had prioritized saving and paying off their student loan debts; as a result, they were in a good position to afford their first home and make a comfortable down payment.

Jamie initially assumed their new Westville friends and peers were at a similar life stage and in a similar socioeconomic situation; after all, birds of a feather tend to flock together. As he and Beth met more new couples in the town, however, he couldn't help but notice an incongruence between their new friends' career paths and their lifestyles. Soon, he realized that many of the people he thought of as contemporaries were benefiting from an invisible hand.

The Duncans, one of the first couples whom Jamie and Beth befriended in Westville, were the perfect example. Jamie met Sam Duncan on their rec-league soccer team, and after Jamie shared that he was new to town, Sam suggested they grab dinner with their significant others. Sam's wife, Emily, and Beth quickly hit it off, and the couples became fast friends.

Sam had recently graduated from an MFA program and was in the process of crafting his first novel, while Emily worked in fundraising for a nonprofit. So when Jamie and Beth received their first invitation to the Duncans' house for brunch, Jamie was surprised to discover that Sam and Emily lived in the extremely expensive Stone Creek community.

"Hey, Beth, did you know the Duncans live in Stone Creek?" he had asked at the time.

"Yeah, I remember Emily mentioning that," Beth replied.

Every Sunday, the developers of Stone Creek ran a full-page ad in *The Boston Globe*, showcasing new homes, and Jamie had become very familiar with the pricing of homes in the different developments. Even though he and Beth were well positioned financially, he was aware that homes in Stone Creek were well beyond their means. Based on what he knew of their occupations, Jamie didn't see any obvious way the Duncans could afford to live there, either.

This impression was confirmed when they arrived at the Duncans', where they walked up stone stairs toward a four-bedroom, four-thousand-square-foot home. Based on the listings he'd seen, Jamie estimated that it cost at least $1,500,000. He also noticed Emily's shiny new BMW X3 SUV in the driveway. At face value, a more than million-dollar home and a top-of-the-line car seemed a little out of the price range of an aspiring author and someone in nonprofit fundraising.

As Jamie gaped at the house, Beth could tell where his mind was going and seemed to preempt him.

"Jamie, don't judge. You don't know their story," she reminded him as they rang the bell.

Two months later, the Duncans invited Jamie and Beth to join them for a weekend at the Cape Cod home of Emily's parents. Prior to their arrival, Jamie and Beth pictured a quaint seaside cottage; what awaited them instead was a sprawling estate in Falmouth, complete with a dock, a tennis court, and a boat named *Prosper*. As they would learn that weekend, Emily's father ran a $10 billion hedge fund in Boston called Patriot Capital.

On Saturday morning, Jamie and Beth lost their doubles match to Sam and Emily, 6–4, 6–3. Jamie was privately frustrated—he had taken the match quite seriously and was visibly perspiring—but Beth seemed less invested in winning and barely seemed to break a sweat, including on some crucial points. Upon returning to the guesthouse where they'd slept the night before for a pre-brunch shower, Jamie and Beth found that the Duncans' maid had already cleaned their room and changed the sheets. The experience felt as luxurious as a stay at the Four Seasons, but Jamie was uncomfortable rather than impressed.

Despite the beauty and opulence of their surroundings, he felt out of place and sensed Beth felt the same, especially after seeing how at ease their new friends were in this environment. Staying with the Duncans felt very different from hanging out with Jamie and Beth's friends from Brighton or Cambridge. While those friends also liked nice things, they took pride in their self-sufficiency and generally lived far more modestly and practically.

The weekend did resolve the mystery of the Duncans' lifestyle. Plainly, they were highly subsidized by their families' wealth. Jamie also noticed that in subtle ways, Sam and Emily seemed to feel it was important to portray themselves as wealthy, even though it was clear that at least a significant portion of the money was coming from their parents. Their pride over their HGTV-worthy home. The sparkling new BMW SUV Emily drove around town. Even the invitation to her parents' vacation estate felt like a gesture of friendship, but also a subtle attempt to showcase their resources. Jamie also observed how the Duncans spoke to the help at the estate, as if it were their house and their staff rather than Emily's parents'. When Emily asked the caretaker at the home if he would mind giving her car a vacuum and a wash when he had a minute, Jamie winced inwardly.

Jamie could not articulate why the Duncans' lifestyle irritated him so much, but it did. He didn't feel jealous of the Duncans. Quite the opposite: something about how they lived felt wrong to him, as though they were missing something fundamental about what it meant to build a life for themselves. He couldn't imagine ever wanting something similar for Beth and himself or for their future kids. Having always worked for everything he had, living lavishly off family money felt like…cheating.

Over time, Jamie came to realize the Duncans weren't

an isolated case. Many of the young couples they met had recently purchased homes in Westville and clearly could not have afforded them on their own merits or means. Not too long after their weekend trip to Cape Cod with the Duncans, Jamie and Beth had met another couple, the Franklins, who'd mentioned offhand at a party that they'd recently made an all-cash offer on their new house to win a bidding war. Beth, while rarely judgmental, was so taken aback by the comment that she brought it up to Jamie as they drove home from the party, remarking, "How do a bookkeeper and a marketing manager come up with that much cash?"

Jamie didn't hazard a guess in response. The answer was obvious.

Over time, the examples continued to pile up. While Jamie and Beth liked most of the people they met in Westville, Jamie could not help but notice how a subtle sense of entitlement permeated aspects of the town's social fabric.

He started to have doubts about his and Beth's plan of raising a family in the community.

On occasion, he shared his observations with Beth, trying subtly to gauge her feelings, but he also tried to avoid overemphasizing his misgivings because he believed she was truly happy in Westville. Beth was positive, adaptable, and understanding; she was instantly well liked and had developed a core group of close friends. He didn't want to uproot her again without a strong justification.

To be fair, Beth occasionally expressed reservations of her own. Once, following a girls' night out, she recounted a story that had struck her as odd. The group had been drinking pretty heavily, especially for a Thursday night. After two and a half large espresso martinis, one of the married women in the group, Rebecca, started complaining that she had barely seen her husband in weeks due to all his work travel before making a veiled insinuation that her "needs" were being met elsewhere.

For a moment, Beth thought she might have misunderstood, but as the conversation continued, Rebecca joked sloppily that she knew her husband "had something on the side, as well."

While Rebecca's candor caught Beth off guard, she was even more surprised to see that Rebecca's admission didn't seem to provoke any disapproval or even discomfort among the other women in the group. They accepted it without batting an eye. Given that everyone at the table was either married or in a serious relationship, Beth had expected at least some subtle pushback or disapproving glances, but she detected neither. Beth didn't consider herself prudish or naive and she recognized that every relationship was different and complex, but she was taken aback by what appeared to be a high level of acceptance of infidelity among the group. When Jamie heard the story, he was similarly surprised.

Westville checked so many boxes for Jamie and Beth. The town was crisscrossed with scenic paths for biking and beautiful hiking trails, which the couple made use of nearly every weekend in the spring, summer, and fall. It also had a charming pancake house that they visited almost every Sunday morning and talked about bringing their future kids to one day. But it seemed like every week,

Jamie had an experience that made him wonder whether it really was the right long-term choice for them.

Jamie constantly weighed the pros and cons of Westville in his mind. On this occasion, still frustrated after his earlier meeting with Matt Embers, he found himself dwelling primarily on the negative.

That all changed when he pulled into his driveway, saw that Beth had beaten him home, and remembered their dinner plans. He swung the car into his parking space and hurried into the house to avoid the cold. After removing his coat, hat, and gloves, he found Beth in the living room with a big smile on her face. She had picked up their favorite Chinese food, the smell filling the room, and lit a roaring fire, which she knew Jamie found relaxing.

"How'd it go today?" she asked, an inquiring look on her face.

Jamie let out a small sigh.

"Long story. Let's eat, and I will tell you." He decided his gripes could wait until he'd helped himself to his favorite boneless spareribs.

As Beth and Jamie sat down for dinner, he began to tell her about his first formal performance review with Matt Embers earlier that day.

The meeting had started positively, with Matt speaking warmly about how Jamie had stepped up in the director role and maintained the trust and respect of his clients after Stacey's departure. He also complimented Jamie for meeting all his performance goals for the quarter and closing several large new project upsells. As a result of these accomplishments, Jamie had earned his full bonus for the year and was on track for a decent raise.

After highlighting these positives, however, Matt had moved on to share a few areas where he felt Jamie had room for development and improvement. This was when the discussion started to take a downward trajectory.

First, Matt reminded Jamie to bill any time overages and expenses to the firm's clients as opposed to the internal client development account; apparently, he still harbored some resentment about Jamie's decision on the Rocket account a few months back.

Another situation Matt raised was a $15,000 write-off incurred during a campaign for another of Jamie's clients, Kendall Scientific. Kendall had agreed to pay fifteen influencers $1,000 each for their campaigns, but a Jones associate had accidentally set the campaign budget to $2,000 per influencer. This error meant the campaign ran $15,000 over budget before Jamie noticed and rectified the error.

Kendall was a new client with significant promise, and Jamie did not feel comfortable billing them for his team's mistake. Instead, he proactively approached the client, admitted the mistake, assured them they would not be charged for it, and emphasized that it would not happen again.

Matt did not support Jamie's solution. The extra $15,000 budget had generated more influencer activity for Kendall, and they had ultimately benefited from this additional exposure, so Matt insisted the client should have been billed for the full amount.

On a pragmatic level, Jamie understood Matt's reasoning, but from a relationship standpoint, he couldn't square the circle. He hadn't avoided billing for the overage just to be nice. His goal with every client was to build a long-standing collaboration, and Kendall had the potential to develop into $100K per-month account. Foreseeing this, Jamie had carefully considered potential upsell plans to pitch to Kendall once he'd fully earned their trust. In his view, he was playing the long game, and billing Kendall for the unexpected overage risked the success of that long-term plan for a short-term gain. He was annoyed that Matt couldn't see the merit of his decision.

Unfortunately, that wasn't the end of the critical feedback. Next, Matt brought up an interaction between Jamie and a managing director at Jones, Sarah McEvoy.

During a sales review meeting, Jamie shared that he believed one of Sarah's clients was a particularly strong fit for an influencer campaign and wanted to pitch the upsell opportunity. He even offered to join Sarah in co-pitching the idea to the client.

But as soon as he'd made the suggestion, Jamie sensed that Sarah felt he was overstepping. She looked around awkwardly, then claimed it would not be a good idea for someone outside her team to pitch the client. Instead, she asked him to provide a few slides for her team to present to the client themselves, without his involvement.

Although he knew it was impossible to convey the benefits of an influencer campaign thoroughly in a PowerPoint, especially when the person presenting wasn't familiar with the channel, Jamie did as he was asked. As he anticipated, the client passed on the opportunity. When Sarah gave Jamie this news in an email, his response revealed some of his frustration.

"Thanks for letting me know. I'm sorry it didn't work out and wish I'd had a chance to present the ideas to help get it over the finish line," he wrote in his reply.

According to Matt, this exemplified something Jamie needed to improve—he needed to show more deference toward the firm's managing directors.

"I know you just wanted to close the deal," Matt said.

"But if an MD makes a call, it's your job to follow their lead. That means staying in your lane."

Privately, Jamie knew his email to Sarah had been a bit passive-aggressive. But he didn't understand why Matt, with his obsession with the bottom line, couldn't appreciate Jamie's efforts to land additional revenue that was clearly there for the taking. This was especially puzzling since no one had provided a valid reason for Sarah, who had minimal experience with influencer campaigns, to present the opportunity. As far as Jamie could tell, she had put her ego ahead of what was best for the business. *Wasn't there something on the lobby wall about "Winning as a team"?* he thought, although he kept this observation to himself.

The final point Matt wanted to discuss and the one that raised Jamie's blood pressure the most was Jamie's handling of one of his former account managers, a top performer named Jessica Sherman.

In November, Jessica shared with Jamie that she had been accepted for early admission to Emory University's business school for the following fall and was planning to attend. She and Jamie had a great relationship, and once she knew she would be attending, she felt dishonest hiding this information from Jamie. She asked whether she could stay at Jones through June, then take the summer off before school.

Coincidentally, Jamie had watched a TEDx Talk titled "It's Time to End Two Weeks' Notice" just a few days before Jessica made this announcement. It inspired him to think differently about how people left companies, and he saw Jessica's situation as a good opportunity to put that new thinking into practice. Jessica was a valuable account manager, and Jamie's team was already short-staffed, so in his eyes, it made perfect sense to allow her to stay on. He told her she was welcome to work through June and that he appreciated her trusting him enough to be candid about her plans. Jessica had continued to excel in her work since then, and Jamie thought it was a win-win scenario.

Matt, however, took a different view. At the performance review, he told Jamie he should have let Jessica go as soon as she told him she would be leaving Jones.

"We really don't want people on our team who aren't 100 percent on board with us. And while it sounds like Jessica is still doing fine, in my experience, people almost always start to lose focus when they've got one foot out the door," Matt explained. "Whatever happens, it's a risk. Letting them go immediately is tough to do, but it's the right call."

Up until that point in the conversation, Jamie had accepted Matt's critiques politely and amicably. But in this case, he couldn't hold back.

"I don't understand what that accomplishes, Matt," Jamie protested. "Jessica is going back to school, not to a competitor, and she has a lot of motivation to finish here on a high note. She also trusted me enough to give me plenty of lead time so we aren't left shorthanded. She could have sat on this for months. Most importantly, she's continuing to do great work, just like always."

"If she doesn't want to be here, she shouldn't be here," Matt countered. "We've got applications coming in the door every day. We're better off opening a slot for someone we know is all in."

Jamie's irritation boiled over, and he slipped into an agitated tone that he had never previously used with a superior. "Oh, come on, Matt. She wants to get her MBA. It has nothing to do with us. She really stuck her neck out being honest about her plans, and for that, I should show her the door?"

Matt was impassive. "I hear you, Jamie. But this is just not what we do," he declared. "It sends the wrong message."

Jamie wanted to interrogate that statement and ask what exactly was wrong about sending the message that it was acceptable to do great work, provide a generous notice period, and leave to pursue attractive opportunities for professional development, but he felt he already knew the answer. The company ruled, employees were expendable, and trust and loyalty at Jones were a one-way street.

Mercifully, this was the last item on Matt's agenda; he concluded the review, thanked Jamie for his time, and congratulated him again on the great results overall. Jamie felt like a cartoon character with steam shooting out of his ears, but he didn't get the sense that Matt had any idea how upset he was.

As Jamie finished recounting the story to Beth, he felt as if he were back in Matt's office, his frustrations mounting and his heart rate clearly elevated, while the screen on his Apple Watch flashed the question: "Did you start a workout?"

To his consternation, Beth didn't seem to entirely comprehend his distress.

"Why are you so upset, Jamie?" Beth asked. "I know you disagreed with some of Matt's feedback, but your numbers were good, you got your bonus, and it sounds like he was mostly positive about your overall performance. I mean, leaders have to make uncomfortable decisions every so often, right? Isn't that part of your new role as a director? Plus, everyone always needs feedback about where they can improve."

For a moment, Jamie was close to losing his temper with Beth. He was already hovering dangerously close to a boiling point, and she seemed more interested in helping Jamie make peace with Matt Embers than in validating his frustrations.

But then he realized even he didn't completely understand why he was so upset. He took a deep breath as he tried to step outside his frustration and be a bit more reflective. After considering what was truly bothering him for a few seconds, he continued in a calmer and more collected tone.

"I've always been fine with feedback. In fact, Stacey regularly gave me very direct feedback about where I could improve and grow," Jamie noted. "But this was different. The areas where Matt wants me to change aren't really about leadership or management. I don't feel like he wants me to improve my skills or tactics so that I can become a better leader, just that he wants me to change the way I do things. Now that I think about it," Jamie said, then paused as he searched for the perfect words, "everything he told me today was an example of judgment...or character."

Until that moment, Jamie hadn't realized what bothered him so much about Matt's feedback, but this was it. This was the root of the problem.

"You feel like he wants you to change who you are," Beth said reflexively.

It was somewhere in between a question and a statement, but as soon as the words left her mouth, Jamie knew instantly that Beth had gotten right to the heart of the issue. As he replayed the discussion in his mind, going over the moments that nagged at him most strongly, they coalesced together: the issues Matt was bringing up were fundamentally questions of values.

"Exactly!" Jamie said. "I always want to get better at my job, but I don't want to change who I am or what I believe is right to appease my company or boss. All the things Matt wanted me to do, if I'd done them, it wouldn't have felt right."

"So what can you do?" Beth asked. Then, with a trace of concern, she added, "I mean, you're not thinking of quitting or anything, right?"

Jamie was going to clarify that he had no plans to leave

Jones. But before he even began to answer that question, his phone rang. It was Chloe Hitchcock.

"Beth, do you mind if I grab this? Chloe is calling me back, and I could use her advice."

"Not at all," Beth replied, knowing how much Chloe had helped Jamie with his career and vice versa.

As Jamie put in his earbuds, stood up from the table, and walked into the office to start the conversation, he saw Beth putting the remaining Chinese takeout into containers to take to work the next day. That was one thing Jamie and Beth always agreed on: there is nothing better than leftover Chinese food.

"So what happened?" Chloe asked, aware Jamie's first review with Matt was scheduled for that day.

Jamie sighed in response. "It's not that it was bad, really. It just isn't sitting well with me," he replied, then went on to recount the entire conversation to Chloe, just as he had to Beth.

The most valuable part of ESML was called Forum, a private group consisting of six or seven people. Jamie and Chloe were part of the same forum.

The stated goal of ESML forums was "to help members grow individually and collectively, both personally and professionally." Each forum met for two to three hours each month outside work hours, giving members an opportunity to present their challenges to a small, trusted circle and receive nonjudgmental feedback in a strictly confidential setting, safely removed from the circles they moved in outside the room.

Jamie and Chloe were the youngest members of their forum and brought both youthful energy and digital experience to the group. Like Jamie, Chloe was a rising star at her company, Compass Media, a full-service marketing and communications agency, and they had learned a lot from sharing their experience and best practices with each other.

Jamie had already told Chloe quite a bit about his previous interactions with Matt. As he shared the story of his performance review, her initial response mirrored Beth's.

"I can see why you'd be frustrated," Chloe empathized. "But you shouldn't lose sight of the fact that it seems like Matt had a lot more praise than criticism for you."

"I just don't know," Jamie said. "The stuff Matt wants me to change just doesn't feel right to me. He wants me to make decisions I would never make if left to my own devices."

This explanation seemed to make sense to Chloe.

"Yeah, I get it," she replied. "No one wants to change who they are just to placate their boss."

"I can deal with Matt," Jamie summarized. "But I can't change what I believe or what I value."

As he said the words, Jamie realized that he and Matt disagreed on many values-based decisions, perhaps more than he had openly acknowledged thus far. Chloe's next question got right to the point, as always.

"Is it Matt?" she queried. "Or is it Jones overall?"

"That's a great question," Jamie replied. "It's hard to say. Stacey and I were always on the same page around these sorts of things, and she was a superstar at Jones for many years. Of course, she did eventually quit."

Chloe seemed to be processing what Jamie was saying or simply giving him more room to speak. Either way, she remained silent, so Jamie continued, changing tack and revealing another reason why he had sought Chloe's counsel.

"Anyway, I was thinking back to the presentation you gave to our forum in September. I'd be interested in digging into it more," Jamie said.

He was referring to a standing element of each ESML forum meeting, where one of the group members gave a presentation about a challenge, problem, or best practice, and other members responded by sharing related stories from their own experiences and asking questions. Chloe had led the most recent exercise, which Jamie found himself ruminating on after his meeting with Matt.

In the forum, Chloe had shared her experience from Compass's latest leadership retreat, where she'd done an exercise to discover her personal core values. One of

Compass's philosophies, she had told the group, was that its leaders should have clarity on who they are and align their leadership style around their core values to lead more authentically and effectively.

The company's founder and CEO, Jack Reardon, led the multiday leadership off-site personally and individually coached each attendee. He had made it clear that Compass wasn't looking for cookie-cutter leaders; instead, it wanted to help people develop their own authentic leadership style and approach.

During her presentation, Chloe had shared a brief overview of the process and the work she had done as part of the training, including her initial list of five personal core values, which now sat on her desk.

- Be grateful for what you have.
- Do your best, always.
- Be self-aware.
- Take ownership.
- Be part of the solution.

When Jamie first saw the list, he thought that those values described Chloe to a T and articulated what made her successful both at and outside work.

As Chloe explained to the forum, having clarity around her values had really helped her develop as a leader and make better decisions—both personally and professionally—even in a short period of time. As a result of this clarity, she had chosen to double down on certain relationships and commitments while cutting back on others. In confidence, she shared some examples of these changes with the forum, including the decision to break up with her boyfriend of four years, who struggled with gratitude, self-awareness, and taking ownership generally, but especially in their relationship.

Chloe had also shared how the exercise had helped her to see how well aligned her values were with both her employer and the people who worked at Compass. In their time attending the forum together, Jamie had often heard Chloe talk about the core values at Compass; they seemed far more tangible and real to her than the hollow words printed on an office lobby wall were to his experience with Jones.

Jamie continued, "I have a sense that I have strong values, but I can't clearly articulate what they are. Do you think you could share the materials from your training with me?"

"I'd love to help," Chloe responded, "but I'm still learning this stuff myself, so it might be the blind leading the blind. Also, I don't know whether I'm supposed to share the materials outside the company."

Jamie was disappointed, but he understood Chloe's position and appreciated her integrity.

Still, Chloe sensed his disappointment.

"Actually, I have an idea," she offered with a sudden burst of enthusiasm. "Let me follow up with you about it in the next few days, I promise."

Jamie could picture the energetic smile on her face, one she wore whenever she was about to solve a problem. When something was important to her, Chloe always found a way to make it happen; maybe, he reflected, her core values of "take ownership" and "be part of the solution" were coming through.

Chloe needed to jump off the call to attend a work dinner, so that was the end of the conversation for the time being. Jamie was encouraged by her support but still felt uncertain about what to do next, so he decided to wait and see what Chloe had up her sleeve.

With that intention in mind, he did his best to put the frustrations of the day behind him and settle into a relaxing evening. He and Beth watched a movie together, after they finally found one they could agree on, and he fell asleep relatively easily.

The next day, Jamie took the commuter rail to work and enjoyed an ordinary day in the office.

He and Matt had a good chat about client priorities and a big client expansion opportunity.

He had a few productive client meetings and gave a new client pitch.

As he settled back into business as usual, Jamie felt the strife from the previous day gradually fading away.

In fact, the day was pleasantly devoid of surprises—that is, until Jamie rode the commuter rail home that evening. As he scrolled through the unread emails on his phone, one stood out. The subject line read, "Core Values Help?" and the sender was Jack Reardon, the CEO of Compass Media.

For a moment, Jamie wondered whether his eyes had misled him, but then he read on:

Jamie,

Chloe told me that you're interested in learning more about your core values. Any friend of Chloe's is a friend of mine.

Would be happy to help. Let me know if you want to grab a coffee this Sunday.

—Jack

Jamie was stunned that Chloe felt comfortable asking the CEO of her company to assist him. He was also surprised that Jack had referred to Chloe as a friend rather than a colleague and had immediately reached out without even knowing Jamie personally.

Everything about the interaction felt alien in comparison with Jamie's experience at Jones, but he was excited to seize the opportunity. He responded right away, and he and Jack agreed on a plan to meet over coffee that Sunday at a diner in Jack's hometown of Arlington, Massachusetts. When he arrived home and told Beth the story, Jamie still couldn't quite wrap his head around what just happened.

3

THE QUESTIONS

Sunday arrived in the blink of an eye, and Jamie felt a pang of excitement and nervousness as he arrived at Victoria's Diner, which he would later learn was an institution in Arlington.

Although Arlington was just outside Jamie's former home of Cambridge, he had only ever driven through it. He noticed that the city center radiated a similar old-world charm as compared to Westville, with the difference that the restaurants appeared a bit older, and many advertised themselves as family owned. Jamie also noticed a large number of families out walking with their kids, even on a winter morning. Many houses still had lights up from the holidays. Something about the town just felt warm and welcoming.

Jamie hadn't wanted to walk into his meeting blind, so he'd done some homework. The previous day, he'd spent a few hours scouring the Internet for everything he could find about Jack Reardon.

He learned that Jack had founded Compass nearly twenty years prior and built it into a successful midsize agency. The company was widely recognized for both its blue-chip client list and award-winning company culture and had received numerous awards naming it one of the best places to work in the Boston area. Jack himself kept a relatively low profile, both inside and outside work, and seemed to avoid the limelight. He was fifty-one with a wife and two kids and appeared highly active in the Arlington community.

Jamie had also discovered that Compass Media was one of the key sponsors of the Rodman Ride, the charity bike ride Jamie and Beth participated in each year. The

Compass website featured a group of company employees at the ride, passing a giant check to a charity organizer, and Jamie had noticed Jack in the background, barely visible in the photo opportunity, despite organizing and leading the team. This was the man he had arranged to meet.

A bell clanged as Jamie opened the door to the diner and entered, and he was greeted by the aroma of freshly baked croissants. After scanning the restaurant, he saw the man he recognized from his research, seated casually in a corner booth.

Jack stood up to shake Jamie's hand as he approached the table. He was over six feet tall with a lean frame, well-trimmed salt-and-pepper hair, and a faint stubble—he clearly had not shaved in a few days and didn't give the impression that he was looking to impress anyone.

Jamie was instantly struck by Jack's unassuming presence, which matched what he had seen in the photos. Compass Media was a very successful firm, and Jack was probably worth several million dollars personally. Yet he was dressed comfortably and unassumingly—a Patagonia fleece and jogging pants without a discernible logo.

Plus, the diner was anything but fancy; it was more of a greasy spoon. A note on the menu indicated that it had been family owned for seventy-five years, founded by Greek immigrants. The staff appeared to be mostly comprised of extended family. It was the type of place that served the best breakfast in town along with coffee that was weak and bitter from hours on the burner in a traditional glass carafe. It would not have been a first choice for Jamie and Beth's new friends from Westville, but Jack seemed totally at home in these surroundings.

"Nice to meet you. I'm Jack," he introduced himself, offering a strong handshake.

"Nice to meet you, too. I can't thank you enough for agreeing to meet me on a weekend," Jamie said. Then, a bit nervously, he stated the obvious, "Especially when you don't even know me."

"Happy to help," Jack said casually. "This topic is very close to my heart."

They settled into the booth and exchanged pleasantries. Despite his stature and seniority, Jack expressed considerable curiosity about Jamie, asking him whether he had ever been to Arlington before, where he lived, and how long he'd been in the Boston area. After chatting for several minutes, Jamie realized he'd been doing most of the talking.

Following the arrival of their lukewarm coffees, Jack kick-started the conversation that had prompted their meeting.

"How can I help?" Jack asked.

Jamie paused for a moment, weighing his words. While Jones and Compass weren't direct competitors, he wanted to be careful what he said; he didn't want to offer any critiques that could get back to Matt and the Jones leadership.

"I'm not totally sure where to start," Jamie admitted. "But over the past year, I've had a few experiences in my life and work where I've felt out of place. Things that have just felt…misaligned. I haven't been able to totally put my finger on why or how. But then when Chloe shared with me how she went through this process to discover her core values at your company, I think I started to understand what's missing."

Jack remained attentive and did not interrupt. His facial expressions seemed to say, "Go on," so Jamie continued.

"I know I'm very principled, but I'm not as clear about how to articulate those principles as I know I could be and…" Jamie stumbled over his words, trying to find the right ones to finish his sentence, gazing upward as though they might reveal themselves on the stained ceiling tiles above him.

Sensing Jamie's hesitation, Jack jumped in with a question.

"Jamie, how would you define a core value?" he asked.

Jamie thought about it and replied, "Something you believe in strongly?"

Jack listened and nodded approvingly, almost paternalistically. But his body language was reserved, indicating that he didn't entirely agree with Jamie's definition.

Sensing this, Jamie asked, "Was I close?"

"Close, yes." Jack smiled. "But I think there is an important distinction. A core value is not just something you believe. A belief can be aspirational without being true," Jack explained. "For example, I believe that climbing Mount Everest would be an incredible experience, but I haven't done it, so I don't know for sure whether that is true for me. A core value is deeper than a belief. It's something that captures who you are at your core and what you do. It's a constant for you, not really a conscious choice."

Jamie felt himself nodding in rapt attention.

Jack continued: "Do you have a sense of any of your core values?"

At this, Jamie tried to hide his smirk. Just as he always prepared carefully to anticipate a client's questions before an initial meeting, Jamie—certain he would be asked the question in some form—had spent the past few days thinking about the topic. He had googled "discovering your core values," and although this mostly resulted in lists of keywords or pricey seminars, he had a few themes that came to mind. They weren't as clear and concise as what Chloe had shared, but he still hoped Jack would be impressed by his diligence.

"So I don't know if these are values per se, but I can tell you a few themes that I came up with," he said with a look somewhere between pride and sheepishness.

"That's a good start," Jack offered.

"Okay. Here they are," Jamie began with a degree of excitement. "I like to do things myself. I believe in integrity. I like to plan ahead and think strategically."

Jack nodded and quickly responded with a question. Clearly, this would be a Socratic dialogue, not a lecture.

"Okay, Jamie, let's dive into one of them to start," Jack began. "What does integrity mean to you?"

Jamie had never been asked that question before. He had always thought integrity was self-explanatory, but now that he was asked directly, he had trouble defining it simply or specifically.

He went through a few options in his head before

admitting, "I guess I don't really know. I've always thought of integrity as kind of a given?"

His response started as a statement but ended as more of a question, with his voice cracking slightly at the end, revealing that he wasn't very sure of his answer.

Jack treated it as a question.

"Yes and no," he replied in a tone that reflected both confidence in what he was about to say and a certain humility. "With the concept of integrity in particular, I think people have very different definitions of what it means," Jack revealed. "For one person, integrity could mean always telling the truth. For another, it could mean doing what they say they'll do. And for yet another, it could mean living their life to their highest ability. All those are viable definitions of integrity, but they are still quite different, especially in the context of core values."

Jamie found himself nodding instinctively as Jack's words landed in a deep and reassuring tone. He had always assumed the definition of integrity was universal, but he was beginning to see why that might not be the case.

"We'll talk about this more later," Jack continued. "But it's a great example of why I suggest avoiding one-word core values. They tend to have too many interpretations. To guide your daily actions and decisions, values need to be very specific."

Immediately, Jamie thought of the one-word values emblazoned on the wall of the Jones lobby.

"So thinking about the word integrity again, what does that look like and feel like for you?"

Jamie mulled this question over for a while, peering down into his mug. As he ruminated, his gaze drifted out the window toward a father helping his two kids cross the road. He turned back to Jack.

"I guess if I think about it more, for me, integrity is about doing right by others," Jamie concluded more confidently. "It means having people's backs and being someone other people can rely on."

As he spoke these words, Jamie felt a strange sense of warmth come over him, and it definitely wasn't from the coffee he had barely sipped. He felt a comforting, energizing sensation when he spoke about those concepts, even though the precise nature of the feeling was hard to explain.

"That's helpful," Jack replied, seeming to notice how the look on Jamie's face changed as he gave his answer. Jack's eyebrows lowered, and a smile formed naturally across his face. "Okay, based on what you just said, I'm guessing that relationships are important to you and that you are someone who can be trusted to act in other people's best interests," Jack summarized.

At this feedback, Jamie's smile became more visible and pronounced, and he again felt that warm tingle down his spine, as if he'd wrapped himself in a fleece blanket in front of a fire. Listening to Jack's words felt like hearing affirmations of how he tried to show up in the world.

Jamie nodded in affirmation and said, "Absolutely."

"Good, now we're getting somewhere," Jack remarked. "Let me ask you another question, Jamie. Can you remember the last time you were asked to do something that would damage someone's trust? Or when you've had a conversation with someone who made it clear that they should not be trusted?"

This was easy. Jamie's mind flew instantly to the memory of his recent performance review with Matt Embers, which he replayed like a slow-motion movie in his head. In particular, he recalled how Jessica, his account manager, had trusted him enough to share her plans to go to business school and how Matt had insisted that Jamie punish her for her honesty.

Jack studied Jamie's face carefully, no doubt noticing how quickly the smile on the latter's face was replaced by a frown and a furrowed brow. Jamie broke eye contact with Jack, peering down at the table. His hands, which had also been resting comfortably on the table, clenched slightly as his fingers slid closer to his palms.

"I sense that you thought of something specific," Jack observed with a look of curiosity and mild satisfaction.

"Yes!" Jamie exclaimed, agitated but excited to let his frustration out. "Recently, I—"

Clang! Suddenly, the bell at the front door rang as a family left, shaking him out of his flow. The noise prompted Jamie to hesitate and scan the restaurant, remembering that he and Jack were not alone.

Jamie paused, ambivalent. He was suddenly reluctant to speak poorly of Matt, especially in public.

Jack seemed to pick up on the signals of Jamie's doubt.

"Work situation?"

"Yes," Jamie confessed, relieved at the empathy and yet slightly unnerved by Jack's prescience. Ever since the beginning of the conversation, he had felt almost as though Jack were a step ahead of him, as if he were playing chess in Jamie's subconscious.

"Why don't you leave out the specifics and just explain the circumstances without any names?" Jack offered.

Jamie observed this potential new mentor closely. He didn't get the sense that Jack was trying to trick him or scrounge up dirt. Instead, Jack emanated a calm, reassuring demeanor that reminded Jamie of his favorite college professor. Though Jamie barely knew the Compass founder, he sensed that he could trust him, at least with high-level details.

Jamie explained the story, leaving out the names of the protagonists. He shared how he was given the feedback that he should have let an employee go for what felt like an unfair reason. He also expressed some of the sentiments he'd discussed with Beth, how he had felt like he was being asked to alter something fundamental about himself to meet Matt's demands.

"I get it," said Jack. "That is certainly not the way I would want my employees to handle that situation."

Jamie felt a wave of relief. His judgment, which had come under such scrutiny in his performance review, suddenly felt validated.

"How did that discussion make you feel?" Jack asked.

"Terrible," Jamie replied. Just bringing the discussion to mind had raised his heart rate and sense of agitation, and a quick glance at his Apple Watch confirmed that his pulse had quickened to eighty-eight beats per minute, a level usually reserved for a brisk walk.

THE QUESTIONS

"Good," Jack said.

This response confused Jamie, but Jack seemed genuinely pleased.

As their server passed the table, Jack casually motioned for the check, then turned his attention back to Jamie. "Can I give you some homework?" he asked.

"Absolutely," Jamie replied.

Jack slid a piece of Compass Media stationery across the table. On it, Jamie saw five questions, hand-written swiftly but neatly.

1. In what nonwork environments have you been highly engaged, and why?
2. In what professional roles have you done your best work, and why?
3. What help, advice, or qualities do people regularly come to you for?
4. When were you disengaged or demotivated in a personal or professional setting, and why?

5. *What qualities in other people do you especially struggle with?*

"Here's what I would like you to do," Jack explained as Jamie read the questions carefully. "When you have a few hours of quiet time, take out five pieces of paper, and write down responses to these questions. Don't worry about the form of your answers; they can be sentences, bulleted lists, words, anything. Just get as much as you can out onto each piece of paper. Don't censor yourself. It's important that you be as honest and raw as possible. Sound good?"

"Sounds pretty straightforward," Jamie replied with a combination of nervousness and excitement.

"Great," Jack said. "Once you've completed the exercise, shoot me an email, and we'll talk about next steps."

The transition from deep discussion to wrapping things up was rapid yet smooth.

A few seconds later, the server dropped the check on the table. Jamie reached out for it, intending to express his gratitude by picking up the tab, but when he opened it, he saw Jack's nondescript blue Visa card already in there with a receipt ready for him to sign and add a tip. Clearly, Jack had given his card to the waitress before Jamie even arrived.

"There was no need to do that," Jamie said, somewhat abashed. "The least I can do is buy you breakfast to thank you for your time."

Jack let out a chuckle, his first of the morning, as if Jamie's offer were absurd.

"Jamie, first of all, it's my pleasure. And second, this is a home game for me," he replied, alluding to the fact that they were in his hometown. "If you really want to thank me, think carefully about those questions."

As Jack looked down at his watch, Jamie slid the list of questions into his pocket, mentally vowing to give them his full attention.

"Jamie, I apologize, but my son has a ski race today, and I need to head over to the mountain," Jack explained.

"Of course," Jamie said, amused that Jack was apologizing to him.

As they stood up from the table, Jamie, unsure of the nature of the relationship developing between them and not wanting to overstep, said, "Thank you again for your time, Jack. Please let me know how much you charge for coaching." He assumed Jack had better things to do with his time than give out free advice.

Jack shook his head. "This isn't pay for play. Happy to be of service, Jamie."

They both stood up at the same time and walked to the door together. Just before they exited the diner, Jack turned to Jamie with a distinctive grin on his face.

"Jamie, you seem like the type of person who likes extra credit," he guessed.

Jamie laughed and nodded his assent; he had never been shy about being the teacher's pet.

"Okay then. Here's one more question I'd like you to ponder over the next few days or weeks. Think back to when you were a kid. Was there something in your life, a specific moment, when you were entrusted to take responsibility for something or someone that was important, and you failed in your responsibility?"

It was an interesting question, but Jamie wasn't clear how or why it pertained to their discussion about core values.

"I'll think about it," he said. He was a bit uneasy that he did not have a quick answer for Jack.

As he left Victoria's and strolled back toward his car, Jamie had an extra pep in his step, coupled with a sense that he was on an important new path. There was a lot of work to do, but he felt that he was on the verge of unlocking some truths that had eluded him for far too long.

Breathing in the brisk New England air, Jamie realized he hadn't met anyone quite like Jack before. The older man was clearly successful and accomplished, but he carried himself with a deep sense of humility and was highly approachable. He must have achieved many of his business goals in a twenty-year career with Compass but seemed motivated by something else, beyond money or recognition.

The contrast with the leadership at Jones felt suddenly

stark. They had always made it clear that ultimately, business was about the bottom line. Numbers on the page trumped all other concerns. Jamie wasn't even sure whether the CEO at Jones knew his last name. Without even discussing Compass, Jamie could tell instinctively that Jack's motivation as a business leader was different, and he surmised that this was probably why Chloe loved working at the company.

Jamie located his car and began the drive home. On the way out of town, he passed an open house at a cute two-story brick-and-wood colonial with traditional New England touches, including shutters and a weather vane. There were at least a dozen couples with young kids lined up outside, waiting for the open house to begin. Jamie noticed the families chatting happily in the cold, even though they were likely going to be bidding against one another.

As Jamie continued out of town toward Route 2, which would take him toward Westville, he noticed that Arlington had its fair share of large houses and, from the looks of the people walking around, both new and old money, similar to Westville. However, something about the area felt a little more communal and welcoming.

He noticed that even the largest, most expensive-seeming homes he drove past tended not to have front gates or fences delineating the property boundaries. This was the opposite of the new homes in the gated communities in Westville, which were surrounded on three sides by monolithic white fences that unsubtly enforced property lines. Jamie also noticed more midrange Hondas, Subarus, and Toyotas in the driveways than he would have expected, which surprised him when he compared it to the BMWs, Mercedeses, and Audis he typically saw in his Westville neighborhood. The residents of Arlington clearly had money, but they didn't seem as interested in showcasing their affluence to others as his current neighbors.

―――――――

When Jamie arrived at home, Beth had gone out for the afternoon to see friends, which gave him the perfect window to dive into the homework Jack had given him right away. Aside from his own enthusiasm for the exercise, he felt like he owed it to Jack to be thorough.

Pausing only to remove his coat and boots before sitting down at his desk, he pulled out a few pieces of paper as Jack had instructed and began to write out his answers.

1. **In what nonwork environments have you been highly engaged, and why?**
   - *I love mentoring youth from less privileged backgrounds. I particularly enjoy it when they trust me enough to open up and share their full stories.*
   - *Moderating a panel on social media with several local executives for my marketing club in college; making sure my questions were up to par and I had the chance to contribute.*
   - *Helping friends think through their long-term goals and career ambitions.*
   - *Walking in the woods, alone with my thoughts.*
   - *Traveling through Europe for a week by myself*

during my semester abroad in college. Especially enjoyed figuring things out and navigating new places.

2. **In what professional roles have you done your best work, and why?**
   - *When I am trusted to manage and cultivate client relationships and rise to the occasion, such as when Stacey left.*
   - *When I am discussing big-picture goals with clients and encouraging them to think ahead.*
   - *Working with Stacey and the team to brainstorm strategies with clients, especially after a setback.*

3. **What help, advice, or qualities do people regularly come to you for?**
   - *I help people when they are at an impasse with another person and can't understand their opinion or perspective.*
   - *Friends come to me when they are in a new*

relationship and have questions about whether it's the right fit.
- After college, I helped my friends think about their career paths/professional goals.
- I help colleagues at Jones build rapport and trust with client contacts.
- I am good at helping a group to build consensus.

4. **When were you disengaged or demotivated in a personal or professional setting, and why?**
   - When Matt Embers questions my judgment and meddles in my client relationships.
   - When managers harp on everything I do and micromanage me.
   - When I am told to do something I don't believe in, especially if it's related to a client.
   - When I feel people are being overly transactional and short-term-focused.
   - When someone jeopardizes long-term relationships.

THE QUESTIONS

5. What are qualities in other people that you especially struggle with?

- *I struggle with people who are inconsistent and unreliable.*
- *I can't stand people who are deceitful or opportunistic.*
- *I hate overly transactional people—people who only focus on what they can gain from others rather than building a relationship.*
- *People who do what they want without factoring in the effect on others.*
- *I am irritated by people who live beyond their means and are comfortable spending other people's money.*

After about an hour, Jamie looked at his notes and felt like he had made enough progress to take a break from the exercise. As he leaned back in his seat, however, he remembered the bonus question Jack had asked him:

"Think back to when you were a kid. Was there

something in your life, a specific moment, when you were entrusted to take responsibility for something or someone that was important, and you failed in your responsibility?"

For a moment, Jamie pushed himself to think of an insightful answer to this question, but he was tired from sleeping poorly the previous night and an early morning workout, so nothing came immediately to mind. He decided to take a break and return to the question another time.

Instead, as he often did when Beth was out of the house, he turned his attention to his work. Jamie and his team had several important upcoming meetings with different groups at Jones as well as a few key client deliverables approaching. He felt it was his responsibility to have the team well prepared.

Beth returned from her outing around 5:00 p.m. She and Jamie made roast chicken for dinner and picked another movie to watch, which they enjoyed with a glass of wine. As they settled into bed, Beth suddenly remembered Jamie's breakfast meeting.

"Oh right, how was your coffee with that Jack guy?" she asked.

Jamie was still on a high from his conversation with Jack, and he smiled when Beth mentioned the meeting. But to his surprise, he didn't feel like going into detail; he was wiped and ready for bed.

"It was good. He was very helpful," Jamie replied. "I'll fill you in more tomorrow."

Beth followed his cue and didn't ask any follow-up questions, and the two drifted off to sleep.

Jamie had planned to look again at his core-values questions on Monday but found himself stuck in meetings most of the day, the list completely slipping his mind.

He was exhausted on Monday night and fell asleep quickly but awoke abruptly at 2:00 a.m. with heavy sweat and a racing heartbeat. A familiar recurring nightmare, one that hadn't bothered him for years, had suddenly returned without warning.

The nightmare was a flashback to a scene from when Jamie was thirteen. His dad had taken him and his eight-year-old sister, Rachel, to the county fair, which took over the town center every Fourth of July. But as soon as they'd reached the ticket counter, Jamie's dad realized he had left a coupon from the local paper in the car that would have given them 50 percent off their ride tickets.

Rather than taking the long trek back to the car, Jamie proudly told his dad he would watch Rachel carefully and stay right where they were, directly in front of one of the carnival games. Knowing how responsible Jamie was, even at that young age, their dad allowed them to stay put.

"Don't let her out of your sight," he said as he headed back to the car to pick up the coupon. Jamie hardly needed the reminder.

As his dad walked away, Jamie grabbed Rachel's hand to ensure she didn't run off and turned his attention to the game.

It was a classic carnival game where people tried to land a softball in a tin bucket. At first glance, it seemed easy, but the softball was so bouncy that it often caromed out of the bucket, even when a contestant aimed correctly.

The man running the softball game—a genial fellow sporting a backward Red Sox hat and red hair—clearly noticed Jamie watching and asked if he wanted to give it a try. Jamie replied that he would once his dad returned with money and carnival tickets. Hoping to rope him in, the carnival worker stepped up his patter.

"How 'bout a practice throw over heah?" he asked in the thickest Boston accent imaginable.

Jamie couldn't resist. He pulled Rachel with him to the counter and grabbed the ball. After quickly palming it to get a sense of its weight, he picked it up in two hands and tossed it, using his nonthrowing hand to add backward spin. To Jamie's amazement, the ball landed in the bucket, bounced, hit the front rim, and settled back into the bucket. If it weren't a practice throw, he would have won a four-foot-tall teddy bear, which he'd been eyeing up and planning to present to his sister.

"Wow, did you see that?!" he exclaimed, turning to Rachel to see her reaction.

Then, with horror, he realized she wasn't there. Even replaying the moment in a dream more than a decade and a half later, he felt the exact same surge of panic that had hit him the moment he realized Rachel wasn't standing next to him anymore.

"Rachel!" he called frantically, casting his eyes around in search of his sister, but it was hard to hear anything over the carnival music. He vividly remembered the chorus to "Hey Ya!" by Outkast blaring out across the field and completely drowning out his voice.

Jamie raced around the area, diving between the various carnival games as he searched for Rachel. He didn't find her, but he did bump into his dad, who had just returned from the car. Upon encountering Jamie alone and panicked, his dad's typically even-keeled face twisted in worry and exasperation. He didn't even have to ask what was going on; he knew instinctively.

"Jamie, how did you lose her?" his dad asked

incredulously. More than the words, however, what stayed with Jamie—and reappeared vividly in his nightmare—was the look of fear and disappointment that Jamie had never seen before or since on his dad's face.

Fortunately, he and his dad found Rachel within a few minutes. As it turned out, she'd spied one of her friends and, in the split second Jamie made his successful toss, rushed over to say hello. She was fine, and Jamie didn't even get into trouble. Once his panic subsided, Jamie's dad rightly blamed himself for leaving a thirteen-year-old unattended and in charge of a young child.

Although Jamie didn't suffer any direct consequences from the event—his dad hadn't even shared the story with Jamie and Rachel's mother later that evening—the damage was done. Letting his dad down that day and putting his sister in danger after being entrusted with her safety caused Jamie deep pain.

As he awoke from the nightmare, sweaty and filled with anxiety, he felt the same sense of anguish, as fresh as it had been all those years ago. This nightmare had struck him at least a dozen times over the years, though, and he had developed a routine to calm himself down. He pulled out the picture he kept in his wallet of himself and Rachel happily riding the merry-go-round that same day, then read placidly for a while, using his cell-phone flashlight to cast light while Beth slept peacefully next to him with her sleep mask on. Once his heart rate settled down, he too drifted back to sleep, his book rising and falling gently on his chest.

It wasn't until he was dressing the next morning and grabbed his Apple Watch off his desk charger that Jamie noticed his notes from Jack's exercise scattered across his bedside table. In particular, he looked again at Jack's bonus question, which he'd written down and circled for emphasis.

"Think back to when you were a kid. Was there something in your life, a specific moment, when you were entrusted to take responsibility for something or someone that was important, and you failed in your responsibility?"

Jamie suddenly felt the hair stand up on the back of his neck. He knew instinctively that his nightmare was the answer to the question. He wasn't sure whether he was more floored by the revelation itself or by the fact that Jack had known to ask the question.

Jamie still needed to eat breakfast before racing out the door, but he felt drawn back to review his responses to Jack's questions. As he did so, skimming through his answers at the breakfast table and grouping several of them together, something clicked, and everything came together like a puzzle.

- I get frustrated when Matt Embers questions my judgment and meddles in my client relationships.
- I help colleagues at Jones build rapport and trust with client contacts.
- I can't stand people who are deceitful or opportunistic
- I love mentoring kids from less privileged backgrounds. I particularly enjoy when they trust me enough to open up and share their full stories.

As he stared at this new grouping, a pattern stood out from these seemingly disconnected statements: trust. That was it. Trust.

Clearly, this was a quality Jamie absolutely needed in his daily life and work. There were few things he loved more than being trusted, and he never felt worse than when he'd broken someone's trust. He felt a surge of confidence that trust formed the foundation of one of his values.

As he boarded the train, still on an adrenaline high, Jamie fired up his laptop and shot a message over to Jack with the subject line "Homework":

Jack,

Thank you again for your time this weekend. I finished the homework and the bonus question. If you have some time to spare, I would love to review my answers with you.

Let me know what works best. I can meet at your convenience.

Jamie

4

THE DISCOVERY

On Friday afternoon, Jamie felt like the clock was moving in slow motion. After a 4:00 p.m. meeting with his team wrapped up at 5:00 p.m. on the dot, Jamie wished everyone a good weekend, headed down to the lobby, and made the twenty-minute walk to Jack Reardon's office, where they had agreed to meet after a brief email exchange.

When he got up to Suite 401, on the fourth floor, he realized that the office was actually anchored within a larger, shared office space. Jamie gave his name to the receptionist, and she pointed him in the direction of Compass's dedicated space at the far side of the floor, where a set of glass double doors with the Compass logo separated the firm's offices from the shared space. Jamie noticed there wasn't really a dedicated reception area, and the office had more of a start-up vibe rather than an agency atmosphere.

As it turned out, Chloe had been right; there was hardly anyone in the Compass office at this hour. As instructed, he sent Jack a quick email on his phone to say that he'd arrived and plopped himself down in a comfy orange sofa.

As he scanned the office, Jamie noticed a wall between two conference rooms with three phrases cut out in bright-orange wood block letters:

> **Be A Problem Solver**
>
> **Consider The Other Side**
>
> **Long-Term Orientation**

He got up to take a closer look.

Under each of the phrases were index cards that

employees had pinned up over the previous year, recognizing other employees who had demonstrated one of the values. The wall also featured pictures of past employees, recognizing them as winners at the annual Core Value Awards. In each photo, the recognized employee was holding an orange baton, a gesture that Jamie suddenly remembered hearing about from Chloe. Each month, in one of the company's all-hands meetings, the orange baton was presented to one employee by another in recognition of an action that aligned with the company's values.

As his gaze panned across the photos, Jamie was struck by how vividly the core values came to life at Compass and how they were reinforced by the stories on the index cards. By comparison, the display made the generic art in Jones's lobby look even more hollow.

Just then, a familiar voice interrupted Jamie's train of thought.

"Like our core-value wall?"

"Oh, Jack, hello," Jamie replied, trying to hide his

startlement. "I do. I like it a lot. I've never seen a company's values before."

Jack nodded and walked toward him. "Well, core values don't mean much if employees' actions and decisions aren't in alignment with those values. A culture needs to reward the behaviors that it wants," he said in his customary friendly yet slightly professorial tone. "I'm not particularly religious, but I have noticed that this is something religion has historically done very well: incentivize and recognize the behavior it wants to encourage."

Curious to understand more, Jamie inquired, "Are these values that everyone has when they come to Compass, or do people need to adapt to the culture?"

"That's an excellent question, Jamie," Jack responded with a small smile, like a teacher pleased with his star pupil. "I believe people can always improve around these values, but our goal is to find those who live and are aligned to them already," Jack explained. "My experience is that adults are not very likely to change who they are at their core unless they really want to enact a major transformation in their lives."

"So…how do you find those people?" Jamie asked.

"It's taken a while to get it right," Jack admitted. "But over the years, we have developed a list of behavior-based questions for each of our values, along with descriptions for our interviewers of what good and bad answers sound like, so they know what to listen and look for when candidates respond."

"Can you give me an example?" Jamie asked, now very interested to understand how this worked.

Without looking at the wall, Jack continued, "For example, take our value of long-term orientation. If I were interviewing you, I might ask you something like 'Tell me about a time when you were asked to make a short-term work decision that went against the long-term interest of the company or a client.' How did you respond?"

The expression on Jamie's face shifted from curious to stoic. He immediately ran through the billing disputes he'd had with Matt, which he felt risked damaging relationships with clients for the sake of a few thousand dollars. On top of that, he thought about how he was pushed to project aggressive sales figures during the pitching process, even though he knew it was unlikely Jones could deliver on those promises.

Suddenly, without realizing it, Jamie started sharing an example: "I can remember this one project when I was…"

Politely, Jack held up his hand. "Don't worry. This isn't an interview," he assured Jamie. "But you're welcome to tell me the story later if you want, when we have time. Let's head to my office," he continued, motioning Jamie to follow him.

Jack led Jamie down the hallway to a decent-size office. For a CEO, the space seemed fairly nondescript; on Jack's desk, which doubled as a conference table with four chairs around it, Jamie noticed a few family photos. The walls were not adorned with awards, plaques, and photos showcasing the company's success, as Jamie had seen in many of his executive clients' offices; those, apparently, were kept in the kitchen Jamie had passed on the way. Instead, nearly the entire wall space in Jack's office was covered with whiteboards and quotes, with the most prominent hanging above the window opposite the entrance door:

> **How we do anything is how we do everything.**

Jack sat down at his desk and gestured for Jamie to join him. To the latter's surprise, Jack made sure to sit on the same side of the table as he, creating a collegial, informal atmosphere.

"Got your homework?" Jack asked.

"Yes," Jamie replied.

"Perfect. Let's copy what you have onto that whiteboard," Jack instructed, pointing to the whiteboard directly to the right of his desk.

Jamie realized that Jack had written each of the

questions he had given him, including the extra credit question, on a distinct section of a whiteboard.

Jamie did as Jack requested. As he wrote, he felt a flutter of nervousness, wanting to impress the CEO both with his answers and his penmanship.

Once everything was copied, Jack stood up and joined him at the whiteboard. As Jamie watched, Jack scanned the various lists. His face took on a look of seriousness, and he slid into a trancelike state of deep concentration. Occasionally, his face broke into a look of revelation, as though he had had an "aha" moment, followed by a look of perplexity. A few times, he even pointed at various phrases on the whiteboard and moved his finger back and forth, as though he were moving words around the board in his mind.

Jamie sat back in a state of confused awe. He wasn't sure if he was supposed to interject, but for once, he was almost afraid to speak, lest he interrupt Jack's work. Eventually, however, Jack broke out of his laser-focused state and turned back to him with a smile.

"You know, sometimes when I do this exercise, I

know we're in for a long day," Jack noted. "But this—we can definitely make some real progress today."

Jamie grinned lopsidedly, a mixture of pleasure and shyness. He felt as though he had passed some kind of test.

"Okay, here's what's next," Jack explained. "Take this sheet of paper."

Jamie took the handout from Jack's hand. It was printed with a collection of dozens of words, such as *trust, honesty, growth, family,* and other descriptive terms:

Trust	Excellence	Strategy
Honesty	Big-Picture Thinking	Long-Term Thinking
Integrity	Inclusivity	Reflection
Growth	Decisiveness	Relationships
Solitude	Reliability	Self-Reliance
Family	Commitment	Autonomy
Helpfulness	Curiosity	Understanding
	Consideration	

"Are these the words I'm going to use to name my values?" Jamie asked.

"Not quite," Jack explained. "A core value really has to contain more than just a single word. It needs to be distinct, action-oriented, and measurable so you can determine whether you are living it at any given moment. What I want you to do with these keywords is write down the ones that match each of your responses. We're going to see whether similar keywords appear under several responses. If they do, that will help us identify some of the themes of your core values."

Jamie picked up the marker eagerly, but before he could start writing, Jack held up his hand.

"One more thing. For the questions where you've written negative responses, like the one about qualities you struggle with in others, I want you to list keywords that represent the opposite of the examples you've written. In those situations, what qualities are missing? Got it?"

Jamie squinted slightly. Although he was having some trouble understanding what Jack meant, he was embarrassed to ask. He felt like he was in a cooking class with Gordon Ramsay or learning tennis from Serena Williams.

Jack clearly picked up on his hesitation.

"This isn't a test. If something doesn't make sense, just ask, and I'll try to do a better job explaining. In this case, if a bullet describes something negative, you want to list the opposite of that. So for example, where you've written, 'when Matt questions my judgment and meddles in my client relationships,' you want to write the keyword 'trust,' because that's an example of him not trusting you."

"Got it!" Jamie exclaimed, perhaps a bit louder than was appropriate. "Okay, here goes."

Jamie quickly did as he was told, writing several keywords from the sheet under each response category.

1. In what nonwork environments have you been highly engaged, and why?

- I love mentoring youth from less privileged backgrounds. I particularly enjoy it when they trust me enough to open up and share their full stories.

- Moderating a panel on social media with several local executives for my marketing club in college; making sure my questions were up to par and I had the chance to contribute.
- Helping friends think through their long-term goals and career ambitions.
- Walking in the woods, alone with my thoughts.
- Traveling through Europe for a week by myself during my semester abroad in college. Especially enjoyed figuring things out and navigating new places.
- **Keywords:** Helpfulness, Excellence, Curiosity, Reflection, Long-Term Thinking, Self-Reliance, Solitude

2. **In what professional roles have you done your best work, and why?**
    - When I am trusted to manage and cultivate

- When I am discussing big-picture goals with clients and encouraging them to think ahead.
- Working with Stacey and the team to brainstorm strategies with clients, especially after a setback.
- Moderating group meetings and making sure everyone's voice is heard
- **Keywords:** Trust, Relationships, Big-Picture Thinking, Long-Term Thinking, Strategy, Inclusivity

3. **What help, advice, or qualities do people regularly come to you for?**

    - I help people when they are at an impasse with another person and can't understand their opinion or perspective.
    - Friends come to me when they are in a new relationship and have questions about whether it's the right fit.

- After college, I helped my friends think about their career paths/professional goals.
- I help colleagues at Jones build rapport and trust with client contacts.
- I am good at helping a group to build consensus.
- **Keywords:** Understanding, Trust, Long-Term Thinking, Relationships, Decisiveness, Inclusivity

4. **When were you disengaged or demotivated in personal or professional setting, and why?**
   - When Matt questions my judgment and meddles in my client relationships.
   - When managers harp on everything I do and micromanage me.
   - When I am told to do something I don't believe in, especially if it's related to a client.
   - When I feel people are being overly transactional and short-term-focused.
   - When someone jeopardizes long-term relationships.

- When I can see that some people are being excluded from conversations and decisions.
- **Keywords:** Trust, Autonomy, Self-Reliance, Integrity, Long-Term Thinking, Relationships, Inclusivity

5. What are qualities in other people that you especially struggle with?

- I struggle with people who are inconsistent and unreliable.
- I can't stand people who are deceitful or opportunistic.
- I hate overly transactional people—people who only focus on what they can gain from others rather than building a relationship.
- People who do what they want without factoring in the effect on others.
- I am irritated by people who live beyond their means and are comfortable spending other people's money.

> **Keywords:** Reliable, Honesty, Integrity, Relationships, Consideration, Self-Reliance

Bonus. "Was there something in your life, a specific moment, when you were entrusted to take responsibility for something or someone that was important, and you failed in your responsibility?"

- Lost track of my sister Rachel at the fair.
- My dad trusted me to look after her and I let her out of my sight.
- Thought she was lost, my dad was visibly disappointed.
- Did not tell my mom until days later.
- **Keywords:** Trust, Family, Relationships, Integrity

"Nice work," Jack noted. "What exactly is the bullet point about your dad and Rachel referring to by the way?"

Jamie felt a lump in his throat. He felt a bit vulnerable sharing the story with Jack but decided he owed it to him to be all in and honest. Soon, he found himself telling the whole story—the ball game at the carnival, how he'd lost track of Rachel, and the face his dad had made when he saw what Jamie had done.

"So that's the answer to the bonus question. My dad trusted me to take care of my sister, and I failed," Jamie finished.

Jack responded with a kind but serious smile, clearly understanding the magnitude of what Jamie had confided in him. "Thank you for sharing that, Jamie. Now, as you look across this whiteboard, what is the first thing that jumps out at you? What is a keyword or theme that you see over and over? I'll give you a little hint: it was something we discussed at the diner last week."

Jamie skimmed the board, the answer flashing in his mind like a neon sign.

"Trust," Jamie said. "Trust shows up over and over."

Jack smiled the widest grin Jamie had seen from him to that point. "It sure does. So why don't you go to that clean whiteboard next to this one and write trust?"

"Great," Jamie said, feeling a warm sensation as he wrote the word on the board. "So now I give it a name?"

"I like how you are thinking, but let's not get too ahead of ourselves," Jack explained. "I want you to review the list of keywords you wrote under each response and group together the ones that come up repeatedly. Especially if they show up three or more times."

Jamie quickly reviewed his answers, hoping to prove himself to Jack as a quick study. Within a few minutes, he'd written a list of the keywords that were repeated throughout his responses.

KEYWORD THEMES

- Trust
- Inclusivity
- Self-Reliance
- Long-Term Thinking
- Relationships
- Integrity

Jamie stepped back to admire his work, then realized he wasn't sure what time it was and checked his watch. When he did so, it became obvious that he would be home later than he'd told Beth, so he broke off for a moment to send her a quick text. He couldn't help but suspect that she wouldn't appreciate his spending so much time on a Friday night with Jack instead of with her.

By the time Jamie had sent his text, Jack had processed the lists and turned to face him.

"Sorry. Just letting my fiancée know I'm running late," Jamie said.

"Is it okay?" Jack questioned.

Jamie brushed off the inquiry. "Yes, she'll be fine. I'll only be a little later than planned, and she usually goes to the gym after work anyway." He didn't want Jack to think he was being inattentive. "So...," Jamie began, changing the subject. "Looks like I have six core values? Is that too many?"

Jack chuckled ever so slightly. "Jamie, you clearly have a results-oriented nature," he noted. "I know you like to get to the solution, but this is a little more art than science. It helps to go through the process in the right order."

Jamie bit his lip and nodded, embarrassed by his hastiness.

"Now, you may indeed have six core values, but we have some more work to do before we'll know whether that is the case," Jack cautioned. "Also, I've found that having too many core values can make it hard to remember them. And if you can't remember them, they're not very helpful."

"So what's the right number?" Jamie wondered aloud, placing his hands on his hips and scrutinizing his six lists.

"In my experience, three or four is ideal," Jack noted. "Everyone's different, though. I still think we need to cut some items on these lists and combine others. My guess is that some of these themes might actually be part of others or may not rise to the level of a core value. I would encourage you to think about which are nice-to-haves and which are really core to you. Also which of your themes overlap or say the same thing."

Jamie stared ahead, feeling as though he'd been asked to choose between family members. Looking again at the board, he wondered whether he really valued trust more than independence. Integrity seemed like a must-have, but could he really cut long-term thinking? That also seemed like a crucial theme.

Jack seemed to register that Jamie was a bit strained by the exercise and offered him a lifeline.

"Let's go back to a question I first asked you over coffee. What does integrity mean to you? And before you answer this time, I want you to look at it this way: when you think of integrity, what do you specifically *do* to live up to that standard?"

At this prompt, something clicked in Jamie's mind, and he answered clearly.

"Integrity, for me at least, is that other people can count on me," Jamie said. "They know that I'm not going to be self-interested. I'm not going to screw people over. I'm always out to prove that people can—"

"Trust you?" Jack finished for him.

"Yes!" Jamie exclaimed.

"Jamie, there's a reason I asked you for a story about when you'd been trusted with something and let someone down," Jack explained. "I could tell from our first conversation that trust is very important to you. It comes up in a lot of your stories and seems to strongly inform how you interact with the world. Based on this, I believe you need people to know they can trust you, and you need to know that you *are* trusted. Such a strong principle often ties back to a resonant childhood event or experience, which is why I wanted you to think about a potential connection."

Listening to these words, Jamie suddenly felt as though he were in the middle of a therapy session, an unfamiliar yet welcome sensation.

He contemplated Jack's words. "Couldn't the desire to be trusted be innate even without a childhood experience?" he challenged.

"Sure. But after doing this for many years, I've found that most core values have deep roots. They're very often connected to our formative experiences, either positive or negative. With issues and values of trust specifically, these usually stem either from a deeply rooted betrayal of trust or some other powerful incident involving trust during childhood. In this case, I think that when you let your sister out of sight at the carnival, you felt strongly that you had betrayed your dad's trust, which was extremely painful for you. That pain has stayed with you, and it's become a driving force in who you've become as an adult." Jamie shifted slightly in his seat, his expression tightening as he prepared to defend himself. As if sensing the tension, Jack quickly added, "A positive force." Hearing these words, Jamie again felt a lump in his throat. For a moment, he might have been back at the fair, looking into his dad's disappointed face, knowing he had let him down. The recollection was so strong he felt a tear starting to well up in his eye but managed to fight it off.

Jack put a hand gently on Jamie's shoulder. "It's okay, Jamie. More important than revisiting the past is understanding how it impacts the present. This exercise isn't about reliving the guilt you felt that day. It's about understanding that after that day, betraying someone's trust became something you never wanted to do again. As a result, you work hard to be trustworthy and place a high value on being able to trust others. That is a great thing and something you should lean into in your work and life. Understanding this connection with the past is key in recognizing what motivates you today. It also helps explain what inspired you to go into a career where relationships built on trust are critical."

Jamie nodded but felt too emotional to articulate himself in the moment.

Jack continued. "I once had an executive coach tell me that our greatest gifts lie next to our deepest wounds. I'll give you an example. A good friend of mine—a child of a single parent who worked long hours at two jobs to sustain the family—spent a lot of time alone as a kid. As you might expect, that loneliness made for some very difficult childhood experiences."

THE DISCOVERY

"Does your friend resent their parent?" Jamie wondered.

"Far from it," Jack replied. "She is extremely grateful and understands that her parent made huge sacrifices for her and did the absolute best they could under the circumstances. But that didn't change the fact that my friend was lonely growing up. She went on to start an award-winning after-school program that operates in hundreds of schools today, essentially providing for others what she needed most as a child. This isn't a sad story, Jamie. This is an example of someone achieving powerful alignment with their core purpose and using a formative childhood experience to fuel a fulfilling career aligned with their values."

Jamie nodded. He took a deep breath and drew an *X* over *Integrity*.

"I think trust is how I live with integrity," Jamie explained.

"I agree," Jack affirmed. "What else do you see? Is there another theme that could be combined in one or more places?"

Jamie felt he was starting to see the full chessboard now. He took a second look at the list:

- Trust
- Inclusivity
- Self-Reliance
- Long-Term Thinking
- Relationships
- ~~Integrity~~

With an air of decision, he looked at the *Relationships* keyword.

"I think most of the positive experiences I've grouped under relationships could also fall under some of my other themes. For example, I liked working with Stacey and the team to brainstorm because I like being the leader of a group discussion. I like getting everyone involved, hearing what others think, and inviting them into the process. So that's a bit like the 'Inclusivity' theme. Helping friends with their life decisions kind of fits into two categories. I like being trusted to help people with big decisions, and I enjoy big-picture, long-term thinking. Inconsistency also fits under both trust and relationships. It bothers me because inconsistent people can't be trusted, just like people who are deceitful or opportunistic. And people who think about relationships as transactional don't account for other people's needs or feelings."

"Now you are cooking with gas," Jack declared, impressed by Jamie's clarity and ability to think critically about his own values.

Before Jack could even suggest a next step, Jamie was immersed in the work, crossing *Relationships* off the list of themes. Then he remembered Jack's comment about the specificity of core values, and it occurred to him that he could elaborate on the general themes to change them from keywords into more descriptive, unique phrases. By this point, he was completely absorbed in the exercise. Unlike at the beginning of the session, when he had written and spoken carefully to impress Jack, he was now in flow and moving quickly, overtaken by the exhilaration of the exercise.

When he was done, he dropped the marker onto the shelf, as if doing a mic drop.

5

THE VALUES

Jack leaned casually on his desk, admiring Jamie's work. On the board, Jamie had written:

CORE VALUES THEMES

- Trusting Relationships
- Considering Different Perspectives
- Self-Reliance and Independence
- Long-Term Thinking

"Jamie, I'm impressed. This is a really, really good start," Jack said with an approving look.

"What's next?" Jamie asked, eager for more. Then he looked at the time—it was 6:34 p.m. He realized that once again, he'd taken a lot of Jack's time. Changing his tone, he exclaimed, "Oh wow, Jack, I'm sorry. You probably have somewhere to be. I didn't mean to keep you so long."

"All good." Jack smiled. "My kids were off school today, so my wife took them to our place in New Hampshire this morning. I'm waiting out rush hour and usually leave around seven, so the timing is perfect."

"Oh, okay. Great," Jamie said, hoping to hide his relief he hadn't worn out his welcome. But apparently, nothing got past Jack, who observed his slight alarm.

"Don't worry. I still trust you, Jamie," Jack said with a wry smile.

Even just hearing the words made Jamie feel a warm sensation.

"But I actually do think we made some great progress and have reached a natural stopping point," Jack continued. "You've written up some really solid themes here. In all likelihood, they are the foundations of your core values. What you need now is a little more time to reflect and test these ideas out in the real world before polishing them up into core values. Why don't you take pictures of everything on the whiteboard?"

Jamie pulled out his phone and carefully photographed the lists he'd made in response to each question, ensuring none of the words were blurred. Then he made sure his hands were steady and took another photo of the list of core-value themes. As he did this, he saw Jack out of the corner of his eye, rifling through his desk. By the time Jamie had captured the images he wanted, Jack had produced an elegantly designed sheet of paper, which he presented to Jamie.

"I give this to every Compass employee who does this exercise," Jack explained. "What you've got here is a great foundation, but this last step is really important in making sure you've selected the right concepts for you and that you're wording your values in a way that makes them unique and accessible."

Jamie skimmed the handout. It included the questions

he had already answered along with a section dedicated to the Core Validator. He chuckled at the name.

"Okay, so what is the Core Validator?" Jamie inquired.

"That's how you'll pressure-test your values and make sure they're right," Jack explained. "Essentially, the Core Validator asks four questions of each proposed value:

- Can you use the core value to make a decision?
- Does the opposite of the core value cause discomfort if you think about it?
- Is the core value a phrase rather than a single word?
- Can you objectively rate yourself against the core value?

Now, you'll notice the first two questions in the Core Validator are written in orange text, and the second two are written in black," Jack noted. "The first two questions, about making a decision and the opposite of your value, will help you know whether you have the right theme. The other two questions will guide you toward the right phrasing. One of the most common mistakes people make in this process is spending too much time trying to figure out the phrasing before they have settled on the correct theme."

"So I think about each of the themes I came up with today and apply the four questions to them?" Jamie asked, seeking confirmation of the next steps.

"Exactly," Jack said and nodded. "And as you refine them, think especially about how they relate to these three things: your life partner, where you live, and where you work or who you work with. Your core values can help shape your decisions on those big three topics."

His interest piqued by this new information, Jamie saw an opportunity to learn a bit more about Jack and perhaps turn the tables a little.

"Can you give me an example of how values inform the big three?" Jamie asked.

Jack raised his eyebrows and smiled. "I know you

know a bit about Compass from Chloe, and I have a feeling you did a lot of homework before we met," Jack said. "So you probably know I started Compass when I was thirty. You probably couldn't find much about my life before then."

Instinctively, Jamie tried to pretend he didn't know what Jack was talking about, but he quickly realized that would be disingenuous, which felt wrong in that context, so he shrugged and offered a grin. "I did a little digging, sure." He had noticed that Jack's LinkedIn profile didn't even list his work history prior to Compass.

"My first job out of school was at a well-known consulting firm, which eventually went bankrupt and was sold off in pieces. I won't tell you which one, because I don't have a lot of nice things to say about them and I don't like to speak ill of the deceased," Jack noted wryly. "When I got out of college, I had a clear mission: get on the corporate track, climb the ladder, become a director by thirty, and eventually become a partner."

Hearing about Jack's youthful ambitions, Jamie felt a

THE VALUES

pang of recognition and validation. They were eerily similar to his own goals.

"My fiancée, who I met in college, supported me all the way. When I worked late or was away for more than fifteen workdays a month, she would say, 'We won't regret this when we're yachting in Newport in twenty years.' I felt like my path in life was crystal clear. All I had to do was put my head down and grind."

"Did you fail?" Jamie asked, the words passing his lips before he could censor them. Once he'd asked the question, he immediately worried whether it was too direct.

Jack, however, didn't bat an eyelid.

"Worse," he said. "I succeeded."

"What do you mean?" Jamie asked, leaning forward with a bit more intrigue.

"I was promoted to director a month before my thirtieth birthday," Jack said. "My fiancée and I went out to dinner to celebrate, and we ordered foie gras and a five-hundred-dollar bottle of wine. Though frankly, I don't really like foie gras, and I didn't have the palate to appreciate such an expensive bottle of wine. She gave me a Rolex that she probably couldn't afford. Almost a year before the promotion, I had proposed that once I made director, we should start planning the wedding we wanted and set a date."

Jamie felt himself smiling a bemused smile.

"Jack, I'm a bit lost. What was the problem?"

"The problem was I was completely miserable in my job. I didn't enjoy the work or the people I worked with at all, and the environment was both toxic and political. It was also clear to me that the senior partners saw junior people as expendable cogs that they could simply replace whenever they wore out. Now, I don't mind working hard. I had to work very hard to build Compass. However, reaching director didn't provide the euphoria or satisfaction that I had expected. Suddenly, I felt as though I had climbed to within sight of the summit, and I didn't like the view. I started questioning everything I was working for and soon realized that my work wasn't tied to my values. I enjoy building things—elevating people and making a real difference for employees and clients. While the money was great, I felt like it was a devil's bargain and knew that becoming a partner at my old firm would have been the wrong professional mountain to climb."

Jamie nodded solemnly. "I think I get it," he said.

"The problem didn't just lie in my working life," Jack continued. "As I examined what I actually wanted most in life, I realized that my fiancée and I weren't truly aligned. I don't particularly enjoy five-star dining or fancy resorts. I'm happiest camping or traveling the country in my RV. When my fiancée showed me pictures of beautifully designed, lavishly decorated homes with perfectly manicured yards, I always nodded along with her, but I was never really moved. I also didn't see yachting in Newport as the culmination of my life's work or a reason to give up a decade of my life. When she gave me that Rolex, I looked at it and it felt like stolen goods meant for someone else. I never even tried it on. It became a symbol of living in pursuit of someone else's definition of success, professionally and personally."

Jamie was stunned by Jack's candor and self-awareness. After a beat of silence, he asked, "So...what did you do?"

"I did the hardest thing I've ever done," Jack said. "I decided to get off that path and start over. Just a few weeks later, after some tough conversations, my fiancée and I broke up. She was a great person in so many ways, and we had a lot in common—we read all the same books, loved cooking together, took long walks around Boston on the weekends, etc. But in the end, we weren't aligned on the big things, like what we wanted our life together to build toward. Notably, she was all about the destination and the rewards, and I was more interested in the quality of the journey. Much to everyone's surprise, I also quit my job, around a month after the breakup. Thankfully, I had some money saved that allowed me to do that, although less than I would've wanted, because my fiancée and I were not big savers at the time. I started Compass shortly after and met my wife less than a year later."

Jamie felt that lump in his throat again. He hadn't expected the conversation to get this heavy. But he felt a real sense of psychological safety with Jack and decided he was comfortable pressing more on the topic.

"How did you know she was the one?" Jamie asked after digesting Jack's words.

"Because every time we had a serious conversation about anything related to life goals, family, or values, we either were aligned from the beginning or were able to reach a consensus relatively easily," Jack explained. "In the early days of Compass, I also did contract work as a consultant to keep some money coming in. But before long, it was clear that Compass could grow faster if I dedicated all my time to it. I sat down with Anna and told her I wanted to give up the contract work and go all in on Compass, knowing it would require making some meaningful cuts to our expenses and lifestyle to make it work. Even though I could tell she was a bit nervous, she was incredibly supportive. That's just one example. But there are a lot of others, too. I admire and respect the way Anna moves through the world—how she treats people, how she shows up for family and friends whenever they need her, how she cares about helping other people improve their situations. We are different people with many different hobbies and interests, but I've never doubted our relationship for a second because we're always aligned on all the big things," Jack explained with a look of deep admiration and a warm smile spreading across his face.

Then he continued.

"Your partner is one of the big three choices in life that need to be aligned with your values. It's your partner, your chosen vocation, and the community in which you decide to live. In my experience, without core alignment in those key areas, there is little chance of real success or happiness in the long run."

At first, Jamie couldn't muster a reply. Spending ninety minutes with Jack felt like trying to drink from a fire hose of life lessons; he was struggling to absorb it all at once.

"I can't thank you enough, Jack," Jamie said finally, "both for your guidance and for sharing your story. Can I ask you one more question, though?"

"Sure," Jack replied. "Shoot."

"Why are you spending so much time helping me with this when you barely even know me? I mean…" Jamie paused. "I am incredibly grateful for your time and want to pay you back somehow, but it would be helpful if I understood why."

Jack laughed reflexively, and Jamie felt as though a joke had just gone over his head.

"There are a few reasons, Jamie," Jack said in his calm, warm voice. Then he stepped toward Jamie, put his hand on his shoulder, and said, "When we have the time, I'll share my own core values with you. That might help answer your question."

With that, he motioned to Jamie to follow him out of the office and, as they walked together to the lobby, turned off the lights.

"Have a great weekend, Jamie," Jack said warmly. "I am excited to see how the next step of the process unfolds for you. I have a feeling you're on the verge of some pretty significant personal and professional breakthroughs."

As Jamie walked out of Jack's office, he felt a strange sense of duality. His mind was racing with insights, but he also felt a sense of calm and confidence that swept across his body. Although he did not yet have a polished list of core values, he knew for sure that the themes that had emerged on the whiteboard in Jack's office explained a lot about who he was at his core and represented the things that mattered most to him.

As Jamie walked toward the train station, big snowflakes began to fall around him. He hardly noticed. He was preoccupied by the flashbulb memories from his life that kept popping into his head. He felt as though the themes he and Jack had just brainstormed were a lens, and he was mentally overlaying that lens onto his memories as they passed through his mind. As they did so, he visualized a green check mark or a red *X* appearing over each memory, clearly indicating whether the memory was an experience of something aligned to a value or in conflict with one.

One of the memories that flashed into his mind

was navigating a ropes course with his family as a child. Halfway across, he'd gotten stuck between two platforms and found himself panicking, calling to his father to come rescue him. But his father gently refused, instead talking him through how to navigate the ropes and reach the next platform. Jamie remembered how proud he'd felt to make it through the challenge himself and how he'd been even prouder when, next time around, he led his friends through the course.

Another memory that flashed in his consciousness was his frustration when Jones's leadership had called everyone back into the office full-time after the pandemic. At the time, Jamie hadn't been able to understand why he was so frustrated. After all, he was pretty social at work and loved brainstorming with colleagues in person. But now it was clear to him that after their performance over the previous year, he felt that he and his colleagues had earned the right to work independently, and the decision indicated that his superiors didn't trust them.

He envisioned an early date with Beth too, about six

weeks after they'd met. As they sat together in the back booth of a cozy Italian restaurant, Beth had talked confidently about what she wanted from her life: she had a clear vision for a family and financial independence and diligently saved 20 percent of her income each month to meet those goals. Jamie remembered being a bit unsure about Beth the first couple of times they met—the two of them seemed to have different interests—but hearing her speak so enthusiastically about her vision for life was exhilarating to him. They officially became a couple that very same week.

Reviewing these adult memories through the new lens of core values was fascinating, but Jamie found himself even more drawn to the connection between his values and his childhood. As he reflected on how the experience of losing his sister at the fair had gone on to shape one of his values so significantly, he also realized that the person in his life whom he hated to let down the most was Rachel. In fact, this was something he really needed to work on. Over the years, Rachel had occasionally taken advantage of this dynamic, knowing that Jamie hated to say no to her and pushing the limits of his generosity as a result. Beth regularly pointed this out to him, and it had become a source of tension in her own relationship with Rachel. How had he missed that?

As he reached the train station and boarded the train back to Westville, Jamie thought once more about Jack's explanation of the big three—his partner, his career, and where he chose to live. As his thoughts naturally drifted to Beth, to Jones Communications, and then to Westville, he pictured a scorecard in his mind. Until that moment, he had been fully committed to all three, but as he settled into his seat and the train pulled out, he realized that ultimately, he was only aligned in his values to one.

With piercing clarity, Jamie realized he had a phone call to make for a conversation he should have had months ago. He wasn't sure whether he was ready for the consequences of the painful decisions that would follow, but he knew it was something he had to do.

6

THE BIG THREE

"That'll be $14.85."

Jamie fumbled through his pocket, looking for his wallet. To his dismay, he realized it was still at home on the counter, where he had forgotten to grab it before leaving for the diner in Arlington.

Diane had served Jamie dozens of times at that point, and when she saw the look on his face, she knew instantly that Jamie didn't have his wallet. As she shook her head dramatically, he half expected her to crack a joke about forcing him to wash dishes.

"It's fine, Jamie," she said. "You can pay for it next

Sunday. I trust you're good for it." With a smile, she handed Jamie the bag containing his regular Sunday order: two egg sandwiches on croissants with avocado, tomato, and cheese.

With a sheepish grin, Jamie thanked Diane for giving him a break and trotted out the door. He was already excited for the next step in his Sunday routine: breakfast in front of the fire, with the morning paper and a cup of coffee from his new pour-over coffee maker.

As Jamie settled into his car, his phone rang. He smiled when he saw the identity of the caller.

"Hey, boss," he said, "I'm guessing you're calling about the pitch?"

"Jamie, you know I hate when you call me that," the voice on the line responded. "But yes. Do you need anything from me to be ready for tomorrow?"

"I'm all over it," Jamie confirmed. "Pitch is at 9:30, so let's meet at the coffee place right outside their office at 9:00 for a final sync and head into their office together."

As he eased the car into drive and set off for home,

Jamie thought back to the phone call he had made two years earlier, right after he finished the core-value exercise and walked out of Jack's office, which had set a series of chain reactions in motion.

He remembered Stacey had been surprised to hear from Jamie on a Friday night, but she was happy to catch up; the two had hardly spoken since she'd left Jones months earlier.

When they sat down a week later over breakfast, Jamie apprised her of recent developments and asked a question he knew he should've asked earlier but hadn't wanted to know the answer to.

"So, Stacey, why did you really leave Jones?"

With some distance, Stacey had been more forthcoming than during their conversation on the day of her departure. She gave Jamie an unvarnished look behind the scenes at Jones Communication and revealed how she'd shielded him from a lot of corporate politics and drama in the years before her departure—drawbacks Jamie had come to know all too well after he stepped into the director role.

As she shared more and more details, Jamie realized that day that while he thought he was happy at Jones, what he really loved was working on Stacey's team. More importantly, Stacey's leadership and the dynamic of her team were not representative of Jones's culture; rather, they were things Stacey had developed as a counterculture within the larger organization. After Stacey's departure, Jamie had experienced far more of the real Jones Communications culture, and he didn't like what he saw. He thought back to how their conversation had ended.

"Stacey, the day you told me you were leaving," Jamie had asked, "you said you were going to a company where you'd be a little more aligned. What did you mean by that?"

"I was hoping to go somewhere more aligned with my values," Stacey had explained.

Jamie understood instantly.

"Honestly, the longer I worked with Matt and the team, the less I trusted their judgment," Stacey admitted. "Eventually, I realized that staying at Jones would mean that sooner or later, I would have to compromise in ways that went against my deepest values. It was beginning to feel inevitable."

Jamie remembered Stacey's statement hitting like a sucker punch.

Having heard what he needed to hear, Jamie had shifted the conversation to Stacey's new job. She shared that she liked her new organization and especially loved the culture. But she had also confessed to being a bit bored and acknowledged that she missed the fast pace of work at Jones.

"There must be something wrong with me," she had joked. "I miss the hustle of agency life."

They had continued chatting for another hour, happy to reconnect, then parted ways with a promise to keep in more frequent contact. The breakfast left Jamie with a lot of food for thought, and it wasn't long before the tensions bubbling beneath the surface at Jones came to a head.

Barely a week later, Jamie and Matt Embers had had their biggest—and last—confrontation. Jamie and the team had just signed a promising new client and agreed to manage several of the client's existing social media channels. The agreed-on budget was $200,000 a month in total spend, to be deployed equally across Instagram and TikTok. With a standard 20 percent media fee, this meant Jones would be paid $40,000 for managing the campaigns. However, due to a few technical glitches, the team could not get access to the client's TikTok account for two weeks, meaning they were unable to deploy $100,000 or half of the monthly paid social budget.

Jamie made the decision not to bill the client for the $20,000 media fee due for the unspent $100,000. Instead, he asked the team to deploy the extra $100,000 the following month and defer the accompanying agency fees until the Jones team had actually done the work to justify the contracted fee.

The client appreciated Jamie's equitable solution. Matt Embers did not.

It was the last month of the quarter, and the $20,000 Jamie deferred affected Matt's department's quarterly bonus pool, which was tied directly to client revenue. Although it wasn't a huge number, it made a significant difference in one specific area, dropping the department's bonus pool from the highest possible tier to the second level.

When he realized this fact, Matt pulled Jamie into his office and told him he should go back to the client and explain that they needed to bill for the contracted amount, even though the work was not yet delivered.

Jamie had half expected this dressing-down. Until that point, he had responded to these types of requests by gritting his teeth, agreeing to do what Matt said, and then agonizing over it later—often during dinnertime rants to Beth.

But this time, something had changed.

Shortly before that meeting, Jamie had collected all the notes from his session at Jack's office and spent several hours with the Core Validator tool, refining his values. After a few emails back and forth with Jack to confirm he was on the right track, Jamie settled on a definitive list of four core values that felt deeply right. Jack had even encouraged him to rank them hierarchically so that he would know which value had the highest precedence in his decision-making in the case of a conflict.

THE BIG THREE

At Jack's recommendation, Jamie had assigned an icon to each value, printed them out on a laminated piece of paper, and placed the list on the desk of his home office for easy reference. His values were:

- Relationships Built on Trust
- Self-Reliance
- Including All Perspectives
- Long-Term Orientation

Relationships Built on Trust

Self-Reliance

Include All Perspectives

Long-Term Orientation

Then, as Jamie felt a strong tension about what Matt was pushing him to do, he finally understood why. Not only was Matt's request clearly the wrong decision for the client, it violated all Jamie's values simultaneously. It broke trust instead of building it, sent a clear message that Matt wouldn't allow Jamie to reach and act on his own conclusions about what was right, ignored both Jamie's perspective and the client's, and prioritized short-term gain, in the form of the quarter's bonus pool, over a mutually beneficial long-term relationship.

Having worked so hard to get clarity on his core values, Jamie had finally realized it was time to live them. As he sat in the conference room that morning listening to Matt, he wasn't really paying attention to what his boss was saying. Instead, his mind had been considering the various ways that the next few minutes, hours, or days could play out.

There was only one logical conclusion. Growing up, one of Jamie's favorite movies was *Jerry Maguire*; the time had come for his own Jerry Maguire moment. He had felt a rush of adrenaline and a strong conviction. The confidence in his tone seemed to take both himself and Matt by surprise.

"Matt, what you are asking me to do here and what you have asked me to do many times before this is to make a decision that is not in the best interest of the client, which will damage their trust in me and my team," Jamie said. "You are not empowering me to make my own decisions as a leader, even though I've consistently shown myself to be someone who does right by our clients and gets results. You are not listening to my perspective at all. On top of all that, you are asking me to prioritize a short-term bonus of a few hundred dollars over the firm's long-term relationship with a potentially very valuable client."

Matt was momentarily taken aback by Jamie's firm, resolute tone and unprepared for such a well-laid-out counterargument, so Jamie continued.

"What you are asking me to do is wrong. I'm afraid I just won't do it," Jamie declared emphatically.

Matt was clearly agitated. At first, Jamie thought Matt

might scream at him. But to his credit, he composed himself before responding deliberately.

"Jamie, I do understand what you're saying," Matt replied. "And I hope I've been clear in expressing how valuable you are to the team here. But I am drawing a hard line here. I'm really not asking. As your manager and leader of this department, I am telling you this is what we need to do. And your job is to execute on that decision, no matter what your feelings on it might be."

Jamie responded quickly, keeping his voice calm yet steely.

"Matt, I don't think you're hearing me," he stated firmly. "I am done making decisions that go against my values, and I won't continue to be a proxy for behavior that I believe is wrong. If that's your final decision, you can tell the client yourself, because I resign, effective today."

Jamie had never seen Matt at quite such a loss for words. It appeared Jamie had caught him totally off guard, unsure what to say next.

Jamie continued.

"Matt, I care about relationships, trust, and doing the right thing. I would offer, both to you and formally to HR, to give Jones a few weeks' notice, allowing me to wrap up my work and properly onboard whoever is going to step in," he explained. "However, we both know that's not how business is conducted here. So I'll save everyone the trouble of going through the motions. I'll pack up my desk and be on my way by the end of the day."

At these words, it clearly dawned on Matt that Jamie wasn't bluffing.

"Jamie, I think we got a bit far afield here. Are you really sure you want to do this? You have a bright future at Jones," Matt reminded him. He pivoted to a conciliatory tone, perhaps hoping this would invite Jamie to rethink his decision.

"Actually," Jamie said, looking his former boss dead in the eye, "I've never been surer of anything in my life."

With a shrug, Matt admitted that Jamie was correct about how things would go down once he let HR and the partners know that Jamie was leaving and declined Jamie's offer of notice.

"Well, this isn't what I expected, but I suppose I can't change your mind," Matt said with a clear undertone of disappointment. "I guess we're done here."

Jamie thanked him for his time and walked out of the conference room, leaving Matt to figure out how to pick up the pieces.

Just a few hours later, after saying good-bye to some of his colleagues and friends, Jamie walked through the Jones lobby for the last time. As he passed the wall displaying the firm's core values of *Clients First* and *Integrity*, he reflexively and audibly chuckled aloud, feeling relieved to know it was the last time he'd have to walk past those hollow words. As he settled into his car and prepared for the drive home, he felt pulled in two different directions. He was confident he'd made the right choice and elated with his decision. At the same time, he knew it would be a big shock to Beth, especially considering her craving for stability, and he hoped she would support this course of action. Their wedding was mere months away, and they'd talked for years about their plans to buy a home and start a family shortly after they married. Now all those plans seemed to be in jeopardy.

Jamie had a feeling he was in for a long night, and that intuition turned out to be entirely on point. His relationship with Beth would never be the same.

As Jamie had anticipated, Beth was initially shocked that he had made such an important decision without consulting her. In particular, she was worried about their carefully-laid-out plans for the future, fearing that Jamie may have burned a major career bridge. For his part, Jamie had been terrified to tell her the news, but he simply had to trust that their relationship could survive his making a choice that was deeply connected to his values.

"Why would you do something like this without talking to me first?" Beth asked, still processing the news. "Especially now, in the middle of everything we have going on and planned?"

It was more than a fair question.

And that was when he told her everything: the full details of the exercise he'd done with Jack, his list of core values, and the clarity that had become available to him when he was finally able to articulate them. It was, without a doubt, the deepest conversation they'd ever had, one that included plenty of tears and stretched late into the night but concluded with what he hoped was a renewed sense of mutual understanding. While Beth was incredibly empathetic, it was a lot for her to process, and it was clear she'd need time to take everything in.

Just two days later, Jamie's cell phone had rung from a number he didn't recognize. He almost always ignored calls from people who weren't in his address book, but something about the number felt familiar, so he took a chance and picked up.

"This is Jamie," he answered.

As soon as Jamie heard the voice on the other line, he immediately realized why the number was familiar. It was in the email signature he'd gotten to know so well over the past few weeks.

"Jamie, it's Jack Reardon," Jack said. "I heard through the grapevine it's been an interesting week for you?"

Chloe had clearly shared the high-level news with Jack, so Jamie wasted no time giving him the full unabridged story of his discussion with Matt.

"You know, Jamie, there's no point in identifying your values if you aren't going to use them," Jack said. "I would tell you that you made the right decision, but I think you already know that. I'll cut to the chase," he continued. "I have an idea that I want to run by you. I think it could be very interesting. Can we meet to discuss?"

Less than twenty-four hours later, Jamie found himself in front of the familiar whiteboards in Jack's office at Compass. But instead of using the whiteboard to puzzle over Jamie's values, the two of them were energetically laying out plans for a new social media and influencer marketing group at Compass.

While they were reviewing the list of capabilities and services they had agreed were necessary to introduce the new practice to Compass's existing clients, Jamie remarked to Jack that the planned scale of this new practice made it more than a one-person job.

That's when it hit him. "I have someone you should meet," Jamie said, a grin lighting up his face. "This person is a great fit with Compass's values."

A few weeks later, he, Stacey, and Jack had sat together in that same office, putting the final touches to the press release that would formally announce Compass's new practice to the world, with Stacey heading it up as senior VP and Jamie as director.

As he headed home with his breakfast that Sunday morning, Jamie reflected on the fortuitous sequence of events that had been set in motion following his call to Stacey and the twists and turns that had ultimately led him to this blissful morning.

As he pulled into the driveway, he waved hello to Max, his new neighbor, who, despite being in his seventies, was busy bagging up his leaves and lining up them up in the driveway.

Jamie admired how active Max was for his age. He also respected that, from what he could see, Max did most of his own yard work. One would never guess that before retirement, Max had been a successful CEO for nearly twenty years. In contrast, Jamie wasn't sure whether any of his old friends from Westville even owned a rake or a leaf blower.

"Jamie, my boy. Got the regular from Victoria's?" Max inquired.

"Of course," Jamie responded, waving the bag. "I was barely able to resist eating mine on the way home."

"How's the wife doing?" Max followed up.

"She's great," Jamie said. "We just had another ultrasound, and everything looks good!"

"Too bad she can't ski this winter," Max noted. Max and his wife owned a ski condo in New Hampshire and had hosted the Hyneses for a weekend the previous year.

"Yeah." Jamie smiled. "I will have to make some day

trips to get a run in. We will be back to New Hampshire next year."

"The three of you!" Max exclaimed, showing genuine excitement about Jamie's impending fatherhood.

Jamie smiled broadly in response, appreciating his neighbor's kindness and warmth. "Yeah, you will have to help pick out his first pair of skis," he said, then wished Max well and hopped over the threshold of the front door. "Back with breakfast, babe," Jamie called out as he took his boots off.

He walked into the living room, where Beth was putting another log on the already roaring fireplace.

When he saw her, Jamie reflected again on how much their lives had changed since that night when he'd told Beth he'd suddenly quit his job at Jones.

That conversation had unlocked a new level of honesty in Jamie and Beth's relationship; everything was finally on the table. He remembered one of the last things he said to her before they drifted off to sleep.

"You and I are really different in a lot of ways," Jamie

had said, holding Beth's hand. "We've often joked about that. But what this has made me realize is that we always seem to be in alignment on the most important things. We both prioritize trust and relationships. We both care about hard work and taking care of ourselves—even down to being financially disciplined and prudent. We both share a similar long-term vision for our life together. I know my decision today feels risky, but I am convinced staying would have been an even bigger risk. I know we will figure this all out."

Then, without even intending to, Beth said the words that validated Jamie most: "I trust you, and you are right. We will figure it out. We always do." Jamie had never heard words that meant more to him.

The next morning, they had called Beth's parents and had an honest conversation about the wedding they really wanted. While her parents were initially a bit disappointed, they were ultimately understanding and accommodating. Jamie and Beth also talked about making a better effort to spend time doing things that the other enjoyed. Beth committed to sign up for ski lessons the following winter, and Jamie suggested they take sailing lessons together on their honeymoon so that they could spend more time on each other's passions.

The next night, fueled by the vulnerability they'd revealed to each other the night before, Jamie and Beth had another long talk. That was when they both had decided that Westville, for all its demonstrable perks, was not where they wanted to live and definitely not where they wanted to raise a family. They both acknowledged that Westville's residents just did not feel like "their people," and Beth revealed that though she'd been reticent to complain about her neighbors, she shared many of Jamie's reservations.

Of course, when Beth said, "So if not Westville, where?" Jamie hadn't been sure.

But that uncertainty vanished a few weeks later. Before Jamie officially signed on to join Compass, Jack invited the couple over to his home for brunch. This was something Jack did with all his senior hires so that his wife, Anna, an impeccable judge of character, could also give her stamp of approval.

After a pleasant brunch, Jamie and Beth found themselves walking around downtown Arlington for the rest of the day. They spent time in the large town center, browsing in the locally owned stores, and they even wandered into a couple of open houses, where they chatted with other families. Over dinner that evening at a local restaurant, Beth looked up at Jamie and said what he had been thinking the entire meal up until that point.

"I could really see us living here, Jamie. It feels like our people."

"I could not agree more," Jamie replied, choking back a tear of appreciation that he and Beth seemed to be on the same page about everything important lately.

Shortly after they were married, they purchased a house in Arlington. As they settled into the community, they knew immediately that they had made the right choice and sensed they shared numerous values with the community, despite the diverse nature of many of their neighbors. A few months later, they made the decision to start a family.

All those changes had led Jamie to that wonderful Sunday morning, settling next to a warm fire with Beth as they prepared to eat breakfast. Jamie was happier than he had ever been before: everything in his life finally felt aligned. Having clarity on his values allowed him to double down on certain aspects of his life and pull back from those activities that weren't in alignment.

As Jamie unwrapped his egg sandwich, he had one final flashback: he thought back to his conversation with Jack right before he signed his offer to join Compass.

"You know, Jack," Jamie said, "you never did tell me why you spend so much time helping people with their core values."

"It's a fair question," Jack admitted. "Many years ago, I did this core-value discovery work for myself. I realized that my dominant core value is 'help others reach their full potential.' Then, as I began to work with our new managers, I consistently found that understanding their core values was crucial to developing their authentic leadership style. We can't lead other people effectively until we fully understand ourselves, Jamie. And as our managers became better leaders in our business, I often heard that they also became better partners, parents, friends, and mentors outside it. This made it clear to me that for so many people, core values were the missing piece of the puzzle in reaching their potential. For every person I help to discover their own values, I feel that I am really living out my own values."

Jamie sensed he had tapped into an emotional current and decided to dig a little further.

"I'm curious, Jack. Does that core value of potential come from something formative in your own life?" Jamie had inquired with a warm grin.

Jack laughed.

"Well, well, the student has become the teacher," he replied. "Let's just say no one ever called me an overachiever when I was in middle school or high school. I lost count of the number of times authority figures in my life told me I wasn't living up to my potential. When I did finally realize what I was good at, I overcompensated by climbing the wrong career ladder as fast as I could, chasing the wrong objectives and working with the wrong people. It wasn't until I was building Compass and growing a team of talented young people that I really felt like I was doing the work I was meant to do and helping people avoid my own mistakes. But that's a story for another time."

Staring at the fire, Jamie suddenly realized that he and Jack never actually finished that conversation and made a note in his calendar to ask him next time they had one of their regular one-to-ones. Then he brought his thoughts firmly back to the present and sat down next to Beth by the fireplace. He was excited to take the first bite of his breakfast sandwich, gearing up for another round of baby-name negotiations that he was destined to lose.

7

THE LESSON

*If you don't have a moral compass,
you will swim in chaos.*

What do you value most in life?

It's a simple question but one that is not easily answered. It's fashionable to talk about values in life, but very few people can clearly articulate exactly what it is they value.

Simply stated, core values are your most important nonnegotiable principles.

You might not be able to name them yet, but they are

always with you and have likely been driving your behavior, consciously or unconsciously, for most of your life.

When you have a gut feeling that something you're doing feels wrong, that's likely a sign you are violating a deeply held value. Similarly, when you are in a moment of flow, doing work you love and barely noticing the passage of time, that's probably a sign that you are acting in alignment with your values.

These core values serve as guideposts, or "swim lanes," that guide you toward the right things and away from the wrong things in your life. The key is having the awareness to do this proactively.

Here's an analogy: imagine driving an expensive sports car through a pitch-black tunnel. Without being able to see the yellow lines on the road or the walls of the tunnel, you'd inevitably run into one of the walls, creating a horrible scraping sound and causing considerable damage. Instinctively, you would pull away and steer back toward the middle before likely overcorrecting and hitting the other wall. This process would repeat itself until you reached the other side of the tunnel, at which point you'd probably panic over the massive car repair bill in your immediate future.

Now, imagine repeating this exercise in a brightly lit tunnel. As long as you are a decent driver, you probably won't veer anywhere near the walls; the yellow lines will guide you away from the dangers on both sides and toward the middle. The lines are your values, and the light in the tunnel is the awareness that comes with knowing what those values are.

Your core values are not aspirational traits, nor are they marketing slogans aimed at presenting you in the best possible light. When identified correctly, they describe who you are and likely who you have always been. Therefore, articulating them is a process of discovery, not invention or self-optimization. You are looking for the instruction manual for your personal operating system, a manual you have never received…until now.

Clarity on core values becomes a powerful decision-making tool, applicable to the day-to-day dilemmas that shape your personal and professional life. Mastering these everyday choices builds a strong foundation, preparing you to tackle life's most significant crossroads with a newfound confidence and integrity. This foundation is especially crucial in moments when core values come into play most strongly—during the most important decisions in your life, the ones I refer to as "the big three":

- **Partner:** Whom you choose as a spouse or life partner.
- **Vocation:** Your chosen career or place of work.
- **Community:** Where you choose to live and the people with whom you surround yourself.

Throughout this story, Jamie navigates his personal big three. In my experience, as you saw with Jamie and Jones Communications, if these big three decisions are not aligned with core values, they turn out poorly. And given that these are probably the most important decisions that you will make in your lifetime, you really want to get them right, ideally sooner than later.

Your values don't need to be identical to the values of the people you work with, your close friends, or even your partner. But even if you aren't in total unison, it's crucial to be in harmony. If one of your core values features generosity, for example, it's a pretty safe bet that you will never feel whole in an environment or relationship defined by selfishness. In fact, you will probably feel terrible, even if you can't articulate exactly why.

Furthermore, this is not a situation you can habituate yourself to. It's unlikely you will adjust to this type of core-value discord—it will eat at you until either you exit the situation or you force yourself to abandon your values. It should go without saying that the latter outcome is a recipe for ongoing pain or feeling like you've betrayed or failed yourself.

Identifying your personal core values provides a clear rubric to assist you in making your most important decisions—especially the big three. Let's say you are trying to decide whether you and your partner are aligned in the ways that matter most. With the aid of your core values, you will know exactly where agreement is imperative and where there is room for negotiation. If you are trying to decide whether to take on a professional opportunity, you will be able to evaluate whether that role will serve your values or if the company or vocation you're considering might regularly force you to compromise or violate a value. Similarly, when you make a choice about where to put down roots, you will have a framework for picking a community that reflects and reinforces what is most important to you rather than one that makes you feel like you are trapped on an island of people who speak a different language.

This is how Jamie felt in Westville, for all its advantages. In terms of location and amenities, it was perfect; but the longer he lived there, the more he realized that the values of his friends and neighbors weren't aligned with his own and regularly caused him discomfort.

Likewise, his frustrating conversations with Matt

Embers illuminated the gulf between the values that were rewarded at Jones and his own. He loved the work he did and felt passionately about the results he achieved for clients, but what was most important to Jamie was building trusting, long-term relationships, which was entirely incompatible with Jones's culture of prioritizing short-term profits over relationships.

In contrast, while Jamie's relationship with Beth had some areas of concern, their points of conflict were far more superficial. Their different temperaments and interests occasionally caused tension, but Jamie eventually recognized that when it came to the most important aspects of their lives, they were deeply aligned. This is why his relationship with Beth was the only one of the big three to survive Jamie's core-values awakening.

Leading with Values

At some point when I was leading a larger team for the first time, I realized that my leadership style wasn't genuine.

Like a lot of new managers, I emulated many of the

best practices modeled by the finest leaders I'd previously worked for or studied. I was also trying to do the exact opposite of what some of the worst leaders I had the misfortune to work with had done. Some of these practices worked for me, some did not, and some felt entirely unnatural. My leadership style was a patchwork quilt rather than something cohesive and authentic.

I remember one specific instance when people on my team had partied way too hard at an industry conference, leaving them unable to function properly the next day. Knowing I needed to address the issue, I sought the advice of another colleague at the same conference and adapted the iron-fisted approach he advocated. Ultimately, that solution did not sit well with me; right away, I felt like I was running someone else's playbook.

That was a wake-up call. But while I had identified the problem, I wasn't sure how to fix it. There's not really an established route to finding your authentic leadership style—which may be why so few people ever do.

I was lucky enough to receive support that guided

my first steps down this path. In 2013, I attended a small, immersive global leadership training program for around twenty up-and-coming leaders run by Entrepreneurs' Organization in Washington, DC. This program became the impetus for my own core-values journey.

To my surprise, the first few days of the program were not focused on the externally facing leadership skills I was expecting to learn—things like public speaking, running meetings, and setting strategies. Instead, we were pushed to reflect on our own personal principles and determine how they shape and define us as leaders.

The program sparked the realization that I had strong core values that served as guideposts in my life and work, although at the time, I was unable to articulate them clearly. Upon returning home, I spent the next six months working to develop a clear, refined list of values without the benefit of a guide to follow.

During this research process, most of the material I came across consisted of lists of keywords and adjectives that could serve as core values. This was interesting, but it didn't help me to define whether something really was a value. Scanning a list of keywords and picking out ones that felt right didn't seem like a comprehensive process that would produce an actionable outcome.

Eventually, through a great deal of trial and error, I developed a process of my own. Using this process, I created a list of five core values and began to refer to them regularly, especially in the areas of decision-making and time commitments. Guided by these values, I started to double down on things and people in my life that served or were aligned to my core values, and simultaneously, I deprioritized commitments and people in my personal and professional life that were clearly not aligned with those values. This included walking away from relationships that no longer made sense for me and probably hadn't for years.

As a direct result of this realignment, I finally started to reach what I always knew was my innate potential, not only as a leader, but as a person. A few years back, when I listened to someone reading my bio before I gave a speech to an organization, I noticed for the first time that every accomplishment they listed—the awards, the books, the TEDx Talk—all occurred ACVD: after core values discovery.

I firmly believe that this type of core-value clarity is a necessary foundation of good leadership and that getting clarity on core values is especially important for leaders. When you don't know or can't articulate what's most important to you, it's hard to show up authentically for your team and hold people accountable. The patchwork-quilt approach I described earlier—emulating the best leadership qualities you've seen and avoiding the worst—won't be enough to enable you to fulfill your true potential as a leader. Plus, the people you lead won't have a clear understanding of what you expect of them.

In his seminal leadership book *Good to Great*, author Jim Collins defined the highest level of leadership, which he referred to as Level 5 leadership. Level 5 leaders are the transcendent individuals who both change the course of their organization and develop the people on their team into great leaders.[1]

In my experience, Level 5 leadership can only be built on a foundation of authenticity and self-awareness, a foundation that only comes with a clear understanding of one's core values. Level 5 leaders can articulate what's most important to them and use that clarity to motivate and inspire others. Rather than trying to be the perfect combination of other effective leaders, they consistently show up authentically as themselves.

Crucially, Level 5 leaders use this self-awareness of their values to set clear expectations for the people they lead. Their teams know where they stand and what is most important.

Here's a real-world example: if a manager knows that one of their core values is *Build Trust*, they will need to make it clear to their employees that seemingly small things like showing up late to meetings, being inaccessible for long stretches of the workday, or missing an occasional deadline may erode trust on a deeper level than they realize. Without this degree of awareness and the capacity to highlight its importance, the manager might not make their expectations clear, and employees may not understand the impact of their actions, leading to avoidable problems and mutual disappointment.

I'll also offer a personal example: one of my core values is *Find a Better Way and Share It*. As a result, I am unwilling to keep to the status quo when it no longer makes sense. I expect people on the teams I lead to strive to improve both themselves and the business. When someone refuses to try something new or look for improvements, especially when things aren't working well, it's just not in my DNA to accept that attitude. Some people flourish under this style of leadership, while others do not, and it's crucial for the people I lead to know this about me up front. That clarity is extremely powerful, and it pays dividends for me, the people I lead, and the organization.

Defining my personal core values with no road map was an arduous process but ultimately an exceptionally valuable one. Once I had clarity on my values and saw the benefits of that clarity, I became passionate about helping leaders find their own values. I took the self-designed process that led me to my own core values and spent years developing it into a teachable curriculum that we made into an integral part of our leadership training at Acceleration Partners. That curriculum is the basis for what you read in this book, along with the process I will take you through in a moment. Before I do that, however, I want to answer a very common question and clarify the distinction between individual and company values.

Company Values vs. Individual Values

This story focused on how Jamie used his newfound awareness of his core values to navigate the big three—his partner, his vocation, and his community. However, core-value alignment is not just for individuals; it is also for companies. The best organizations have alignment between what they believe, what they say, and what they do.

Company core values represent a shared perspective, distinct from personal core values, which are individually defined. As a result, the discovery process for each is different, and this book focuses primarily on personal core values. If you are interested in that work, I would check out Jim Collins's "Mission to Mars" exercise: it is a great place to start. Then you can use the same Core Validator process described shortly. At the same time, it is still crucial to understand how values, both personal and organizational, influence one's professional life.

Every company has a culture, be it by design or by default. At the foundation of every culture is a set of shared values that guide behavior for leaders and employees alike. Many of us, including myself, have experienced disillusionment with the notion of company values. We have seen hollow values such as *Honesty*, *Integrity*, and *Teamwork* painted on office walls or displayed proudly on company websites. For many organizations, these generic values serve only as virtue-signaling platitudes; they don't actually reflect the behavior of the people in those organizations.

In the now-famous Netflix Culture Deck, former

chief talent officer Patty McCord and founder Reed Hastings clearly pointed out this dissonance.[2] They highlighted how Enron—which had gone bankrupt in a fraud scandal that sent several of the firm's leaders to jail in the early 2000s—had these values displayed in their lobby:

- Integrity
- Communication
- Respect
- Excellence

McCord and Hastings asserted that these types of vague, marketing-oriented values are meaningless—especially when they are not even close to accurate. A company's actual values are illustrated by how people behave when no one is watching, the decisions leadership makes, and who gets rewarded, promoted, or let go. At Enron, employees who lied, cheated, and took outsize risks received accolades, promotions, and bonuses; and people who worked there knew this. The values above, which Enron displayed proudly in the lobbies of their offices, were wall art at best.

In contrast, Netflix wasn't concerned about how their values looked to the outside world. Instead, they crafted values that differentiated them from other businesses, aiming to attract people who found those values appealing. Here were some of the concepts shared in that same deck:

- Adequate performance gets appreciation and a generous severance.
- We are a team, not a family.

These statements would likely turn many people off, and that is exactly the point. They repelled people who wouldn't fit at Netflix and attracted the people needed to build a successful company with an authentic culture. The goal of identifying and sharing organizational core values shouldn't be to please everyone—it should be to create an environment where the right people for the business excel, are rewarded, and feel fulfilled.

A few years back at Acceleration Partners, we had to make a decision about one of our largest clients, who represented over a million dollars in annual revenue. The client was clearly important to our business, but they were also disrespectful and endlessly demanding of our team. In fact, many employees who worked on the account left our company because satisfying the client was just too challenging; the turnover rate on that team was double the average across the business as a whole.

As we discussed our options in a leadership team meeting, someone cited the repeated relationship problems the client caused and stated the obvious: "We know this company violates our core value of *Embrace Relationships*. We just need to decide whether we are willing to take the financial hit."

Put that way, the decision was clear: we fired the customer and openly shared with employees the information that we made the choice based on our core values.

And yes, that decision did have negative financial consequences in the short term. Long term, however, it was absolutely the right choice for the company.

There has been some debate recently around the concept of culture fit, especially in the context of inclusion. It's become more common now to claim that employees should be an "add" to a company's culture as opposed to a fit. While I think there are some semantics at play, I have landed somewhere in the middle on this debate. I agree that it's important to avoid creating a culture that insists on homogeneity, a mistake that almost always results in groupthink. At the same time, I am resolute on the importance of shared values.

You don't need to agree with, act like, or think identically to everyone in your organization all the time. But just as in a healthy personal relationship, you need to be in alignment on the big stuff. To employ a nonwork analogy, no one really wants a vocal atheist in their religious study group. They may like this person and be friends with them despite their different ideas about religion, but in the context of the study group's shared purpose and values—discussing religious ideas and beliefs—there is a clear lack of alignment. Someone who is constantly challenging one of the core values and beliefs of the group will cause ongoing tension and discord.

Most people join a company and quit their manager, so it's especially important for employees to feel a sense of values alignment with both their organization and their direct leader. The trouble is we don't always notice a leader's values when things are going well. Instead, it's often during difficult times, when difficult decisions must be made, that values become apparent and are tested. As Warren Buffett once said, "Only when the tide goes out do you discover who's been swimming naked."

It's not always necessary for an individual's values to match perfectly with an organization's. In cases where the employee and the company are diametrically opposed on values, however—like Jamie being forced to make short-term decisions to maximize profits, going against his ironclad value of *Long-Term Orientation*—it's very hard for the employee to be happy and engaged in the long run. Eventually, it becomes impossible to sustain the dissonance. For everyone's sake, it is better to identify this type of lack of alignment early, which is why personal core-value work is so vital within great organizations.

Starting Down the Path

Now that we've discussed the why and the what of core values, we've naturally come to the how. As mentioned above, I took the self-designed process that led me to my own core values and began to develop it into a teachable curriculum, which we've since used in our advanced leadership trainings with our up-and-coming leaders. Not only has this helped dozens of our leaders define their core values, I have witnessed numerous personal breakthroughs as a result of the process.

Jack takes Jamie through this same process in this book. It starts with asking yourself six key behavior-based questions, designed to identify themes that recur across different aspects of your personal and professional life. There is one additional question here that was not on Jamie's list:

- In what nonwork environments are you highly engaged, and why?
- In what professional roles or jobs have you done your best work, and why?
- What help, advice, or qualities do others come to you for?
- When have you been disengaged in a personal or professional setting, and why?
- What qualities in other people do you struggle with most?
- What would you want said about you in your eulogy?

The next step, as we saw with Jamie, is to write out your answers to each question on its own sheet of paper—six questions, six pages. Once you have a response to each question, identify keywords or phrases that appear repeatedly. For example:

> **Question:** What help, advice, or strengths do others come to you for?
>
> **Answer:** People ask me for candid advice on what they can do to improve. They expect me to share what they need to hear to get better, not what they want to hear to make them feel better.
>
> **Keywords:** Better, Improve, Candor, Coaching

For questions that describe the opposite of your values such as "What qualities in other people do you struggle with most?" you'll want to list keywords that describe the opposite of your responses. If you write that you can't stand insincere people, for example, then *sincerity* or *authenticity* are the best keywords to describe what you value.

Once you've done this for each of the six questions, take out some fresh paper and write down all the keywords that appear multiple times across multiple questions, along with the answers associated with those keywords. The more frequently a theme or keyword appears in your answers, the more likely it is to be part of a core value.

As you group similar keywords and answers, the themes that represent your core values will begin to emerge. Then you can begin to craft each of those themes into potential values.

One of the most common mistakes people make in this process is concentrating too much on trying to perfectly label a core value before ensuring that the theme resonates deeply for them. This is where the four questions in the Core Validator Jack gives Jamie in the story comes into play.

The first two questions in the Core Validator are about selecting the right theme—putting the horse before the cart. The second two are about wording the value in a way that maximizes its usefulness, enabling it to guide your actions.

RIGHT THEME

1. **Can you use your core value to make a decision?**
2. **Does the opposite of your core value cause discomfort if you think about it?**

RIGHT WORDING

3. **Is the core value a phrase rather than a single word?**
4. **Can you objectively rate yourself on it?**

Let's dig into the reasoning behind each of these questions:

1. **Can you use your core value to make a decision?**

    The most important use case of core values is to make decisions, both about how you spend your time each day and how you approach big life milestones. A solid core value should give you confidence that you're making the right choice.

Therefore, if you feel that using a theme that has emerged as a decision-making rubric would give you confidence, especially around a major decision, you are on the right track.

2. **Does the opposite of your core value cause discomfort?**

If something is a value, then the violation of that value will inevitably spark deep negative reactions or feelings. It should feel like kryptonite. This is where it can be helpful to think about the inverse of the proposed value.

When I coach people on discovering their values, I often ask someone to imagine the opposite of the theme as a person at a party with whom they must make conversation. They often wince viscerally as they imagine that person, a sure sign that they're on the right track. A person with a core value of *Relationships Based on Trust*, for example, would really struggle to be friends with or be in a relationship with someone who regularly breaks or violates people's trust. A person who always thinks with the long term in mind would struggle with a partner who spends every dollar they earn and lives for the moment.

If you imagine the opposite of a potential core-value theme and feel immediately uncomfortable, that's a strong indication that the theme is significant for you.

3. Is the core value a phrase rather than a single word?

Many people make the mistake of using single words as their values. For example, many people have told me they have a core value of integrity—an example referenced in the story. The problem is that integrity means different things to different people. For some, integrity means doing what you say you'll do or telling the truth. For others, it means doing right by others. Others may take integrity to mean living according to their principles, which can be very different from person to person.

If your core value is a phrase rather than a word, the extra descriptive words can serve to make it more specific to you. For example, instead of integrity, someone might choose to define their value as *Always Keep Your Word*, which is specific, actionable, and unique to that person. It passes the validator test.

4. **Can you objectively rate yourself on it?**

In addition to serving as a decision-making rubric, core values are also useful in helping you evaluate whether you are living in alignment with those principles. For example, a person with a value of *Relationships Based on Trust*, like Jamie, could reflect on that value in terms of their behaviors and decisions over the past month.

Are they showing up for the most important people in their lives? Are they keeping their promises? Or are they falling short of what they've promised to other people and need to commit to getting back on track? Effective core values can serve as a report card for your life—if you aren't living up to your values, you will feel out of alignment.

Once you've run your list through the Core Validator and feel good about your answers to the four questions, you are on your way to an official first draft of your core values. Now you need to road test them in your life and see how they fare—and how they make you feel.

Write down your list, and keep them somewhere you'll see them every day—such as your desk at work. Send them to someone who knows you well, and ask for their feedback. Over the span of a few weeks, assess whether they help you make decisions. If the answer is yes, you may have created a good list of values. Otherwise, keep tweaking and looking back on the process above until your values effectively serve to guide your decisions.

To better understand the process, I'd also encourage

you to reread Chapter 4, The Discovery, where Jamie and Jack work through the exercise. Now that you have more context on the process, you may find reviewing the back-and-forth of their conversation and following along much more illuminating.

A Final Note

If you have made it this far and are excited about what core-value clarity might unlock for you, the best day to start that work is today. Once you've clarified your values and begin making what you'll likely realize are overdue changes in your life based on them, you will be amazed how quickly things start to fall into place. You will get more done with less energy expenditure, lead from a place of authenticity, and feel comfortable stepping away from commitments and people that no longer serve you and that probably haven't for years.

I would be remiss if I did not warn you that living in alignment with your values is not always easy or painless. Sometimes it requires making difficult decisions that come with a real financial or emotional price tag in the short term. Many people, upon discovering their values, exit professional partnerships and personal relationships to live according to them; in the moment, those breakups can be excruciating. This short-term pain, however, is almost always a smaller price to pay than continuing down the wrong path. In my experience, core-value misalignments that initially show up as fissures or tremors almost always lead to an eventual rupture.

Years ago, for example, one of my children was friends with a kid whose parents' judgment I simply did not trust; there was a clear values misalignment, which I felt in my gut. Our two kids got along really well, though, and I did not want to create any awkwardness that could jeopardize the children's friendship.

One day, my child went on a playdate with the other child. From there, they went on to a pool party. We had not explicitly given our permission for this and would not have. Our child was a relatively inexperienced swimmer, and the party was taking place at a house where we knew a lot of the adults would be drinking and therefore the quality of the supervision would be questionable. As soon as I learned about the new plans, I considered picking my child up but decided against it because it might lead to an uncomfortable confrontation.

My child was more than an hour late being dropped off after the party, and we could not get in touch with the friend's parents. At that point, both my wife and I started to panic. As much as I was worried for their safety, I was also mad at myself for having overlooked what I knew was a clear values mismatch. Fortunately, that situation turned out okay, and no one was harmed, but I thought about that situation for months and vowed to never make the same mistake again.

If you are willing to do the work and make the hard choices, I firmly believe that discovering and aligning with your core values has the potential to take your life and leadership to the next level. It may also help you reach your full potential in a way that has eluded you for many years.

We all start life without an instruction manual or a compass, but this does not mean we have to continue navigating without one. Nowhere is this more true than when it comes to making those big three decisions.

I hope this story has helped you understand the what, why, and how of core values. What comes next is entirely up to you.

CORE VALUES COURSE

If you are excited to discover your core values but still a bit intimidated by the process—or you simply don't want to do it alone—I have a resource to help you.

My core values course contains the full process explained in this book, developed by me and later honed over many years of real-world use with leaders. The course has already helped more than two thousand people discover their core values.

The course is completely on-demand, so you can progress through it at your own pace. After an hour of working on the lessons, you'll have a first draft of your list of core values. From there, the course also comes with twelve weeks of emails, sharing coaching, best practices, and exercises to help you pressure-test and refine your list. I even offer a special option featuring live coaching, which is available a few times a year. Many of the leaders I've worked with have chosen to take the course together with their teams as a professional development exercise.

To learn more, visit **corevaluescourse.com** or **scan the QR code below**. You can also use code "compass" for a discount.

ACKNOWLEDGMENTS

I constantly encourage my kids to step out of their comfort zones, and although she might not remember it, my daughter, Chloe, was a significant inspiration for this book. A few years ago, she challenged me to write a fiction book—something far outside my comfort zone—and later offered some very pointed and insightful feedback on the introduction, showing she's clearly picked up a thing or two from my editing approach to her work. There's something deeply gratifying about seeing the parenting lessons you've instilled in your kids reflected back at you.

ACKNOWLEDGMENTS

I have been passionate about the topic of core values for years and knew I wanted to turn it into a book, but I wasn't sure how. Chloe's encouragement led me to consider the parable format, which was both a challenge and an incredibly rewarding experience for someone who had only written and mostly reads nonfiction. Of course, no creative journey happens in isolation, and I owe so much to the incredible people who supported me along the way.

To my wife, Rachel: After twenty-five years together, it's no surprise that we don't always agree or share the same interests—what fun would that be anyway? But we've always shared the core values that guide our lives and our family. I feel so lucky that, when it comes to the big things, we're always on the same team. There's no one I'd rather navigate life's adventures with, and I'm deeply grateful for the life we've built together.

I've been fortunate to have a team of amazing editors who have supported me throughout this project. Mick Sloan was there from the beginning, serving as a sounding board and editor as each chapter took shape. Rob

Wolf Peterson, as he has done many times before, provided a critical fresh perspective on the final draft, helping to identify areas where my inexperience with fiction was causing confusion for the reader.

Finally, I want to thank Ariel Curry, my editor at Sourcebooks, who jumped in just weeks after joining the team and offered invaluable feedback that brought the book across the finish line.

I also want to express my ongoing appreciation to Alexis Hurley and Richard Pine at Inkwell Management and the Sourcebooks team for supporting my creative vision and taking a chance on a book that does not follow traditional conventions.

NOTES

1 Jim Collins, *Good to Great: Why Some Companies Make the Leap...and Others Don't* (HarperBusiness, 2001).
2 Patty McCord and Reed Hastings, *Netflix Culture: Freedom & Responsibility* (Netflix, 2009).

ABOUT THE AUTHOR

Robert Glazer is the founder and chairman of the board of Acceleration Partners, a global leader in partnership marketing. He also cofounded and chaired BrandCycle, which was acquired by Stack Commerce/TPG in 2021. A serial entrepreneur and award-winning executive, Robert is passionate about helping individuals and organizations elevate their performance.

Under his leadership, Acceleration Partners garnered numerous accolades, including Glassdoor's Employees' Choice Awards, *Entrepreneur*'s Top Company Culture, *Inc.*'s Best Place to Work, and *Fortune*'s Best Small &

ABOUT THE AUTHOR

Medium Workplaces. Robert himself was twice named to Glassdoor's list of Top CEOs for Small and Medium Companies in the U.S., ranking #2.

Robert shares his insights through Friday Forward, a weekly inspirational newsletter reaching over two hundred thousand readers in more than one hundred countries. He is also the #1 *Wall Street Journal*, *USA Today*, and international bestselling author of eight books, including *Elevate*, *Friday Forward*, *Elevate Your Team*, and *Rethinking Two Weeks' Notice*. Additionally, Robert hosts the *Elevate Podcast*, a top 1 percent show on business, performance, and leadership with over four million downloads globally.

His work has been featured in outlets such as *Harvard Business Review*, the *Today* show, *Business Insider*, *Fast Company*, *Inc.*, *Forbes*, and *Entrepreneur*. Robert speaks to audiences around the world on topics of leadership, culture, and personal and professional development and has also spoken on the TEDx stage.

Outside work, Robert enjoys skiing, cycling, reading,

traveling, spending quality time with his family, and overseeing home renovation projects.

To learn more about his writing, speaking, core values workshops, or partnerships opportunities, visit robertglazer.com.